WITHDRAWN

Jessie Minassian's *Backwards Beauty* is a must-read if you have a desire to overcome the bondage of insecurity and body image issues. She is very honest and open about her own battle, making this a captivating and easy read!

KYLIE BISUTTI
Author of *I'm No Angel*

Backwards Beauty is an enjoyable and insightful read. As a mother of a teenager, I found many profound truths and insights of great value in raising (or being) a teen in the very confusing climate of body image today. Excellent book.

CINDY MORGAN
Singer/songwriter, author of *How Could I Ask for More*

Jessie gets it—all the ways we can make ourselves feel ugly and what embracing our God-given beauty looks like. In this open, honest, entertaining book, you'll feel like you are sitting across the couch, under a blankie with a girl who's been there—talking about the power of our words, our dress, and our bodies—and you'll walk away feeling empowered to live a life of true, lasting beauty that grows more powerful—not less—with time. Thank you, Jessie, for using your voice to speak truth to a generation that needs it, and making us l

JENNIFER STRICKLAN
Author of *More Beautiful Tha*

No matter what we look like, for most of us girls, beauty can be the one ugly subject. Jessie tackles the subject of beauty with a unique brand of honesty, transparency, and wisdom. More importantly, she shows us that the secrets to true beauty are found in God's Word. For every girl who wants to feel beautiful, this book is a must-read.

ERIN DAVIS
Author, speaker, blogger

Jessie helps us move toward embracing our true beauty by backing us away from the crazy talk we don't even realize we believe. Listen in, hear yourself, and turn away from lies and toward freedom. Silence the hiss and become be-you-ti-ful you!

ELISA MORGAN
Speaker, author of *Hello, Beauty Full: Seeing Yourself as God Sees You*

BACKWARDS BEAUTY

BEAUTY

HOW TO FEEL UGLY IN 10 SIMPLE STEPS

A Life, Love & God Book from JESSIE MINASSIAN

A NavPress resource published in alliance
with Tyndale House Publishers, Inc.

NAVPRESS⬤®

NavPress is the publishing ministry of The Navigators, an international Christian organization and leader in personal spiritual development. NavPress is committed to helping people grow spiritually and enjoy lives of meaning and hope through personal and group resources that are biblically rooted, culturally relevant, and highly practical.

For more information, visit www.NavPress.com.

Backwards Beauty: How to Feel Ugly in 10 Simple Steps
Copyright © 2016 by Jessie Minassian. All rights reserved.
A NavPress resource published in alliance with Tyndale House Publishers, Inc.

NAVPRESS and the NAVPRESS logo are registered trademarks of NavPress, The Navigators, Colorado Springs, CO. *TYNDALE* is a registered trademark of Tyndale House Publishers, Inc. Absence of ® in connection with marks of NavPress or other parties does not indicate an absence of registration of those marks.

Cover design by Nicole Grimes

Cover photographs are the property of their respective copyright holders, and all rights are reserved. Girl lying in bed copyright © Image Source/Getty; girl in field copyright © letohin/Dollar Photo Club; exotic woman copyright © Paul Hill/Dollar Photo Club; woman with red lipstick copyright © konstandinos/Dollar Photo Club; retro woman copyright © chika_milan/Dollar Photo Club; black woman sitting copyright © kazzakova/Dollar Photo Club; friends' group copyright © Monkey Business/Dollar Photo Club; blonde woman copyright © Studio Kwadrat/Dollar Photo Club; woman with trendy glasses copyright © arthurhidden/Dollar Photo Club; African woman copyright © iconogenic/Dollar Photo Club; young woman copyright © deniskomarov/Dollar Photo Club; beautiful and fashionable women copyright © nuzza11/Dollar Photo Club; girl with fluttering hair copyright © nizas/Dollar Photo Club; woman with stylish makeup copyright © blackday/Dollar Photo Club; woman in gym copyright © Boggy/Dollar Photo Club.

Author photo taken by Open Sky Photography, copyright © 2014. All rights reserved.

The Team: Don Pape, Publisher; Caitlyn Carlson, Acquiring Editor; Nicci Hubert, Developmental Editor

Published in association with the literary agency of Wolgemuth & Associates, Inc.

Unless otherwise indicated, all Scripture quotations are taken from the *Holy Bible*, New Living Translation, copyright © 1996, 2004, 2015 by Tyndale House Foundation. Used by permission of Tyndale House Publishers, Inc., Carol Stream, Illinois 60188. All rights reserved. Scripture quotations marked MSG are taken from *THE MESSAGE* by Eugene H. Peterson, copyright © 1993, 1994, 1995, 1996, 2000, 2001, 2002. Used by permission of NavPress Publishing Group. All rights reserved. Scripture quotations marked HCSB are taken from the Holman Christian Standard Bible,® copyright © 1999, 2000, 2002, 2003, 2009 by Holman Bible Publishers. Used by permission. Holman Christian Standard Bible,® Holman CSB,® and HCSB® are federally registered trademarks of Holman Bible Publishers.

Some of the anecdotal illustrations in this book are true to life and are included with the permission of the persons involved. All other illustrations are composites of real situations, and any resemblance to people living or dead is coincidental.

Library of Congress Cataloging-in-Publication Data

Names: Minassian, Jessie.
Title: Backwards beauty : how to feel ugly in 10 simple steps / Jessie Minassian.
Description: Colorado Springs : NavPress, 2016. | Includes bibliographical references.
Identifiers: LCCN 2015033531 | ISBN 9781612916293
Subjects: LCSH: Teenage girls—Religious life. | Christian girls—Religious life. | Beauty, Personal—Religious aspects—Christianity. | Self-perception in adolescence—Religious aspects—Christianity.
Classification: LCC BV4551.3 .M54 2016 | DDC 248.8/33—dc23
LC record available at http://lccn.loc.gov/2015033531

Printed in the United States of America

22	21	20	19	18	17	16
7	6	5	4	3	2	1

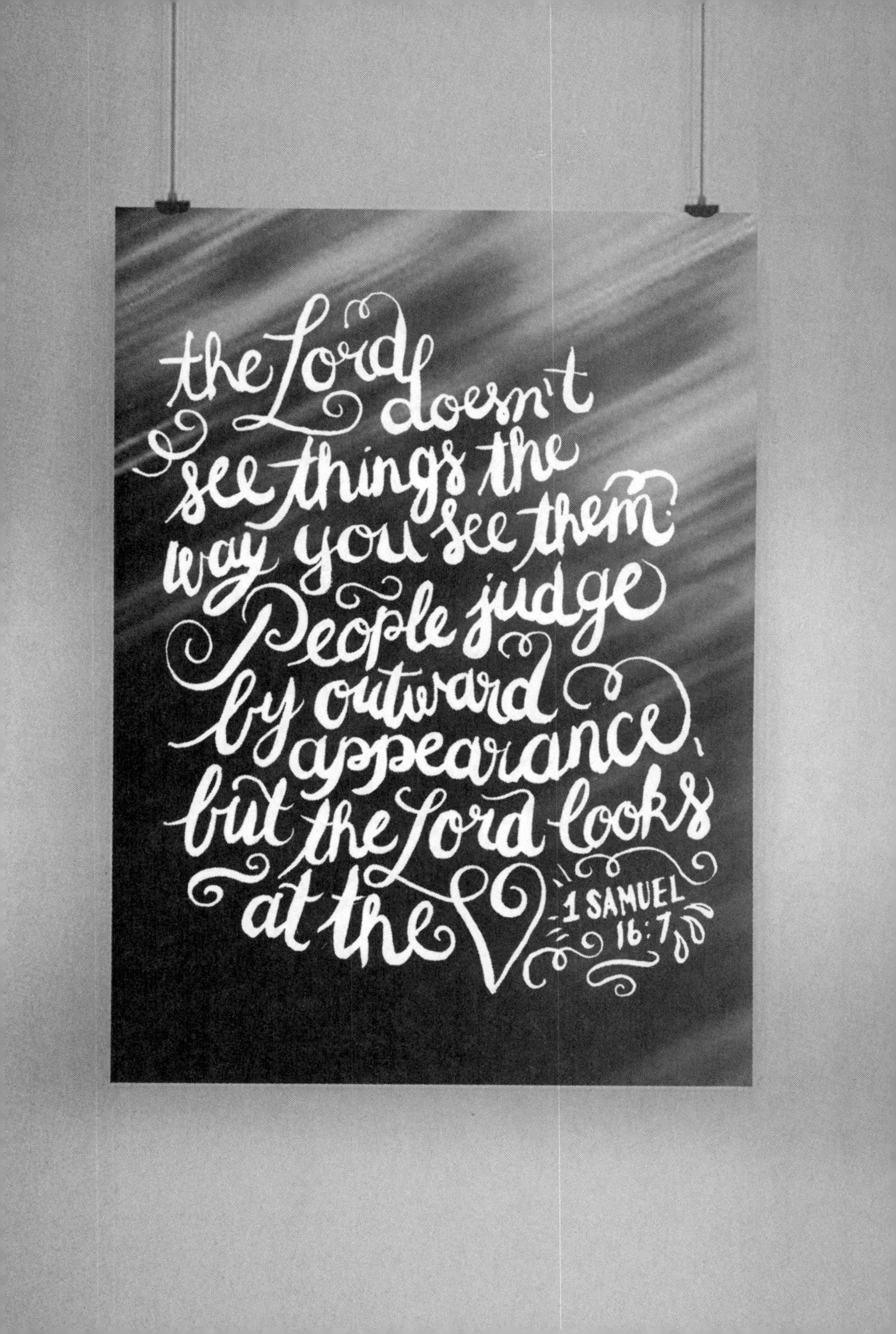
the Lord doesn't
see things the
way you see them.
People judge
by outward
appearance,
but the Lord looks
at the
1 SAMUEL
16:7

To my beautiful daughters,
Ryan Kailey and Logan Cassidy.

May you always know (and believe!)
how perfectly exquisite you are.

Contents

Introduction

I've read a lot of books—*lots* of them—and all my favorites have something in common: Each one made me feel as if I were talking with a friend, or at least someone who cared about my life. I guess when it comes down to it, I don't like having someone I've never met tell me how to live. Wild guess here—maybe you don't either? It's easier to listen to advice when we hear it from someone we know and who we know cares about us, right? (And, let's be honest, sometimes it's really encouraging to hear that an author is *human*, just like the rest of us!) So before we dig into this book together, it's only fair that we get to know each other a bit.

I'm Jessie. My given name is actually Jessica, and my last name is so hard to pronounce that I avoid using it when possible. (Just for kicks, it's pronounced min-à-see-in.) My single momma brought me into this world on a beautiful Californian March day just a *few* years ago (wink). She got married when I was five, and I grew up in a blended family of five kids. I played lots of sports in school and tried to figure out how to love God with my whole heart when it seemed to be *way* more interested in boys. (Maybe you can relate?) I liked school when I had friends, thought it was miserable when I didn't. I got good grades, ate too many Twix for lunch, and never got used to spending ten to twelve hours a week on a school bus. (We kind of lived in the boondocks.)

After high school graduation, I went to a Christian college in Southern California. I played volleyball there and then got into rock climbing. I studied abroad two semesters, one in Israel and the other in Costa Rica. I still liked school when I had friends and learned not to be miserable when I didn't. I got fewer good grades, stopped eating Twix for lunch, and traded the school bus for my first car (a ridiculously small, gold Toyota MR2). There were ups, there were downs, and then there was *him*.

I married my match made in heaven the weekend after college graduation. For now, let me just say that Paul (or "Paco," as most people know him) swept me off my feet and I have never looked back. Best friends make the best soul mates, and he was—and is—both. (*Awww!*) I didn't think I had room for any more love in my heart until God gave us two daughters, Ryan and Logan. They're sweet li'l blessings wrapped in two feisty packages!

Besides loving on my family, my greatest joy these days is to help girls find their identity, pleasure, and purpose in God. I'm the resident big sis for a website called LifeLoveandGod.com, where I answer girls' questions about . . . well, life, love, and God. (I know, pretty creative, right?) Now that I have two daughters of my own, I'm all the more passionate about seeing girls understand their unique beauty, know how amazing God is, and hold their heads high in dignity.

That's where the LIFE, LOVE & GOD series comes in. These

books are meant to be the closest thing to just hanging out at my house, going for a hike together, or meeting for a small group in my living room. Each book covers different stuff you're facing, whether it's relationships with guys, shameful addictions, or getting along with your family.

You'll want to have a notebook or journal handy for the discussion questions at the end of each chapter. Trust me, you'll get so much more out of this book if you take time to think through those questions. Even better if you can grab a couple of friends (or your mom or a youth-group leader) and go through the book together! My heart is to see you grow in your relationship with God and shine with confidence, and that happens most often when you're in community with others.

You can find out more about my random favorite things on the "Meet Jessie" page at LifeLoveandGod.com. I'd love to hear a little about you, too, if you'd like to send me an e-mail through the website!

Now, without further ado, let's get busy giving you the tools you'll need to feel your ugliest! (Wink.)

Love,

Jessie

Kale, Kate, and the Great Longing

A few months ago, an ad for *Shape* magazine caught my eye.

Actually, since it's just us girls here, I might as well be honest: One particular picture of one particular person in one particular *Shape* magazine ad sent me on a mini body-image spiral. Let me explain.

I was on a mad Google hunt for a kale salad recipe. For real. But you know how those searches go: Whatever you start to look for usually gets sidetracked by lots of stuff you *weren't* looking for and didn't really need to know or see. Ever. (It's amazing how many rabbit holes run through that virtual wonderland we call the Internet.) So there I was, feeling pretty good about myself for searching for kale, period. But my determination was sidetracked before my third click.

The person who hijacked my search for a delicious cruciferous salad? Actress Kate Hudson, looking glowing and fabulous and oh-so-trim in her workout clothes. The article claimed that Miss Kate had a revolutionary workout that got her body rockin' like three minutes after the total-body-stretch-and-plump, also known as getting pregnant—a process I'm quite familiar with and have willingly undergone. Twice. (You are welcome, my children.) At this point, maybe I should mention that I've always thought Kate Hudson was beautiful. Really beautiful. Not in an obsessive way or anything. More like a "I sure wouldn't complain if I got mistaken for her twin" kind of way. So when this ad made it sound as though anyone could look just like that golden beauty—even after having kids— by following four simple exercises, I fell for it and clicked through.

So there I was, reading an article I had no intention of looking for, jealous of a woman I will never meet, and later, practicing Pilates moves on my dirty, sticky kitchen floor. I wish I could say my jealous tirade stopped there, but alas, it continued. The article mentioned that Kate had recently launched a new line of workout clothes, which she just happened to be wearing in the photo that had first caught my attention. So now I was on her workout clothes website, admiring Kate in spandex leggings, slouchy hoodies, and neon-colored sports bras. It sounds ridiculous to admit, but I couldn't help but ponder the next dumb question: Would I look like *that* if I wore *those*? It was as if someone opened my head, took out my usually logical brain, and put it on ice while I oohed and aahed at the promised butt-lifting shorts and tummy-slimming tops. I spent way too long browsing the entire "Kate's Picks" page and—as if wasting my time weren't enough—proceeded to waste my hard-earned cash by ordering a pair of black leggings and a camo-print tank top, complete with matching headband.

The clothes finally arrived, and when I tried them on, I didn't magically transform into Kate Hudson—big surprise. Don't get me wrong. They were cute, but my hair didn't spring into golden loveliness, and my booty certainly wasn't any tighter. I was still me: perfectly imperfect Jessie.

To be honest, before celebrating Kate Hudson Envy Day that fateful afternoon, I hadn't been spending a whole lot of time worrying about my looks. I guess you could say that as I've gotten older, I've become more comfortable in my skin (or maybe my skin has just gotten more comfortable as it stretches out). God has done amazing work in my heart and life over the past decade to help me see the beauty that was hiding in plain sight all along. So given my normally steady beat, I was shocked at how quickly I reverted to complete preoccupation with my looks based on one advertisement. My body-image relapse reminded me that every single girl out there—even of the Christian variety—feels the tension of a powerful longing at work in her heart.

The Great Longing

Can I tell you something about me? Something I don't usually start a conversation with?

I want to be pretty.

There, I said it. Does that make me a conceited starlet? An

insecure whiner? A Hollywood wannabe? No, it just makes me a woman. And if you're female, I can guarantee with 100 percent certainty that you want to feel pretty too. How do I know? Because God made us that way.

Let's go back to the beginning. Do you remember the story? God made the sky and the water, the land and the animals, and then on the sixth day He made Adam. He set Adam up in the gorgeous Garden of Eden—the perfect backdrop to start this whole humanity thing—and gave him the job of taking care of all the plants and animals. But even with that lush setting and all those animals, Adam was lonely, and it didn't take long to realize that no lion, tiger, or bear was going to fill his need for companionship. So God put him to sleep, took a rib, and let His divine creative juices flow once again. And the rest is history: Eve was the culmination of artistry, God's final act of creation on planet Earth. And He declared that creating girls was a very good thing (see Genesis 1:31). (Can I get an amen?)

God could have created another Adam, you know. They could have been best bros and had a great time chasing the animals, singing campfire songs under the stars, and having belching contests after dinner. But instead He created something new, something "other." God created Eve very different from Adam. Sure there are those "anatomically correct" differences you learned about in sex ed class, but I'm talking about the more subtle differences that make men and women unique. Here are just a few to get you thinking:[1]

A Guy	A Girl
Has more angular features, from his shoulders to his jaw	Has softer features, from her hips to her skin texture
Has more muscle mass	Has more body fat (which helps shape those curvy lines!)
Has less contrast between the color of his eyes, lips, and surrounding skin	Has more contrast between the color of her eyes, lips, and surrounding skin (makeup boosts that contrast even more)
Is generally larger, from his height to his overall body mass	Is generally smaller, from her arms to her narrower fingers
Is well suited for physical labor	Is perfectly designed for going into labor (like of the baby variety)
Has less hair on his head and more on the rest of his body	Has more hair on her head and less on the rest of her body
Has a deeper voice	Has a higher tone to her voice
Has a visible Adam's apple	Has (what seem to be) larger eyes because of the bone shape below and above them
Has bushier eyebrows that follow a straight line	Has thinner, higher, and more curved eyebrows

Of course, these are generalities, so please don't do the normal girl thing and start comparing yourself to everything in the right-hand column! I've included them only to help you consider some of those unique characteristics about your body that make you distinctly *woman*.

I'm sure you've heard the joke about how the first woman got her name. After God got done turning Adam's rib into a masterpiece, He brought her to Adam for the big reveal. Adam took one look at that hot li'l lady and exclaimed, "Whoa, man!" (Ba-dum-cha.)

Lame joke. But it holds a timeless truth: God made Eve to be Adam's beautiful counterpart. Did you catch that? From our softer skin and captivating curves to our sensitive and nurturing nature, part of our role as girls is simply to be beautiful! How cool is that?

The very fact that God didn't create another Adam says something. God created Eve's body and soul to captivate Adam, to delight him and enchant him.[2] God wanted Adam to find Eve *desirable*. (Kind of helps with that whole "be fruitful and multiply" command He gave in Genesis 1:28.) And here's the really important part we need to understand before we talk about beauty: God gave Eve a *desire to be desired*.

She *wanted* to be wanted by Adam.

A DADDY'S LOVE

Our desire to be loved starts way before our first crush; it starts with our dads. To find out how that relationship (or lack of one) plays into your self-image, decisions, and direction, check out the next LIFE, LOVE & GOD book on the topic of family (coming in 2017).

Fast-forward several thousand years, and you and I are no different. As Eve's daughters, our hearts are wired to want to be the object of a man's longing. We desire to be desirable, just like our Edenic momma. But here's where that desire gets twisted: In the twenty-first century, most of the voices we hear every day tell us that only a very particular *kind* of girl is physically beautiful. And if we don't feel that we match that image of beauty being shoved in our faces everywhere we look, it crushes a little piece of our identity. It's like a knife being shoved into our hearts and twisted. It makes us feel inferior, and we wonder if we'll ever be wanted. Have you ever felt that way? Have you ever felt that because you weren't tall enough or thin enough or curvy enough or smooth enough that *you* just weren't enough? Not just that you weren't as pretty as the next girl but that *you*—as a person, at the core of your being—weren't enough? Well, that's your woman-ness talking. And we need to get a handle on the truth of our beauty and our desirability if we're not going to get owned by our insecurities, especially if we're going to start believing what God says about us.

So first things first. To get to the truth of our beauty, we need to answer this age-old question: Does outward beauty matter?

"It's What's on the Inside That Counts" *(And Other Truths We Pretend to Believe)*

We've all heard it at one time or another. For me it comes like clockwork when I'm looking in the mirror on one of my worst hair days, or when I get a monster zit dead center on my forehead or on the tip of my nose. (Why they always show up in the worst possible places, I do not know. But I digress . . .) From out of the depths of my gray matter, I hear her: my alter ego with a voice reminiscent of a ninety-three-year-old woman looking for her lost poodle. "Now, Jessie," she croons, "just remember: It's what's inside that counts!" If my eyes rolled any farther back, I'm sure I'd see her in the back of my head, knitting booties in a rocking chair, no doubt. And I want to fire back, "Oh yeah? No one's going to *care* what's inside when they get knocked over by this thing protruding from my face, now are they?"

But is it true? Is internal beauty really all that matters?

As we'll see in a minute, God's Word is crystal clear: Internal beauty is priority numero uno. It's definitely *most* important. That said, in real life, statements such as "It's what's on the inside that counts" and "God's opinion matters most" fall flat on hearts programmed to be desirable. And I'd rather wrestle through some hard truths together than give you pat answers. When you feel ugly, hearing "God loves you just the way you are" feels like bailing water from a sinking cruise liner with a thimble.

I think some of us Christians have focused so much on the superiority of internal beauty that we've stifled that God-given longing we have as girls to be beautiful outside, too. Maybe God had Bible writers like Solomon, Peter, and Paul remind girls about the importance of internal beauty because we already had the external part down! It comes naturally to us to care about looking good. I don't think any of us would argue that if left to ourselves, we girls do tend to care too much about looking good on the outside. So God wrote verses like these to remind us not to go overboard on our looks:

> The LORD doesn't see things the way you see them. People judge by outward appearance, but the LORD looks at the heart.
>
> I SAMUEL 16:7

> A beautiful woman who lacks discretion
>   is like a gold ring in a pig's snout.
>
> PROVERBS 11:22

> Charm is deceptive, and beauty does not last;
>   but a woman who fears the LORD will be
>   greatly praised.
>
> PROVERBS 31:30

> Don't be concerned about the outward beauty of fancy hairstyles, expensive jewelry, or beautiful clothes. You should clothe yourselves instead with the beauty that comes from within, the unfading beauty of a gentle and quiet spirit, which is so precious to God.
>
> I PETER 3:3-4

These verses should be scrawled across our bathroom mirrors and posted on our closet doors. We need to memorize them, meditate on them, and let them flow out of our lives! But I also see room for balance. These verses don't tell us we have to choose between *all* internal or *all* external. That's great news for those of us who enjoy mascara, mud masks, and a perfect pair of shoes. We can enjoy being girls and still love God with all our hearts, souls, and minds (which Jesus said is the greatest commandment; see Matthew 22:37-38). Call me crazy, but I think it's possible to be outwardly beautiful while still having discretion, fearing the Lord, and cultivating a "gentle and quiet spirit" (1 Peter 3:4).

We can't ignore the desire God has given us to be desirable any more than we can wish away our uterus. It's just part of being a woman, my friend. So it should come as good news to us that beauty isn't bad. Looking cute isn't evil. Can it become an idol? Absolutely. And we're going to discover how to guard against that in the chapters to come. But there's another reason why we need to treat the pursuit of beauty carefully: Arriving at "beautiful" is next to impossible. In fact, it seems the harder we try to reach our idea of perfect beauty, the less likely we are to see ourselves as beautiful. Interestingly enough, even girls who seem to match society's ideal are not immune to feeling undesirable.

The Harder We Try, the Less We Succeed

Just about every girl on the planet struggles with self-worth and body-image issues, even the prettiest, most popular specimens of our species. One friend in particular stands out as a perfect example of this bizarre phenomenon. The first time I saw Cassidy[3] was during a work meeting, and I was—how do I put it? I think completely intimidated about sums it up. At five foot eight, her slender (but not-too-skinny) frame and tan complexion caught my attention. She had long brown hair, sparkling eyes, and the cutest freckles you ever saw. Cassidy was *beautiful*.

I finally got over my fear that Cassidy would somehow eat me alive and sat next to her one day. Turns out she was the picture of sweetness—a down-to-earth girl with a love for God and a passion for His Word. In time we got to be good friends, so when I started doing research for a Bible study I was writing about body image for women,[4] I asked if I could interview her. Here are a few of her answers:

Q: True or False: I believe I am beautiful inside and out.
A: False

Q: On a scale of 1 to 10, how happy are you with the way you look?
A: 6

Q: True or False: If it had been up to me, I would have made me just the way I am.
A: False

Q: What would you need to change in order to feel completely content with your body?

A: I want longer legs, a smaller nose, straighter teeth, bigger eyes, skin not so ruddy, a body not so flabby, fewer freckles and moles, no spider veins, a chin that doesn't just drop right off into my neck (I have no jawline), olive skin, arms not so hairy, a butt that doesn't jiggle so much, and bigger boobs. I would also like to maintain a slightly thinner frame, and I cannot decide which would be better: a breast enlargement or a nose job.

When I read Cassidy's answers, my jaw just about hit the floor. *Really?* She couldn't possibly be talking about the same person I saw. How could someone so beautiful feel so *not* beautiful?

Cassidy had everything going for her too. Not only was she beautiful, she also had a great job, really nice (supercute) fiancé, and killer personality. Yet this beautiful daughter of the King admitted to struggling with self-loathing. At first glance, it seemed that of all people, Cassidy should be feeling pretty confident about herself. I mean, she checked nearly every box on society's "beauty scorecard." So the fact that even *she* was ready to sign up for a nip, tuck, and plump showed me that none of us is immune. In fact, her honesty hit on an important truth. It doesn't make sense, but here it is:

The more we focus on becoming physically beautiful, the uglier we feel.

Remember, wanting to look beautiful—to be desirable—isn't bad, but we have to be careful. And realistic. The more we focus on becoming beautiful, the further away perfection will feel. If we think we'll be most wanted if we attain a one-size-fits-all image of perfection, we're going to be chasing that proverbial carrot our entire lives. *Always* chasing. Trust me, I know. It's a law of life that I'm quite familiar with, and I have the Kate-Hudson-look-alike clothes to prove it (as well as the emotional scars that came from trying to be something I'm not for much of my life).

Yep, I have a whole lot of experience trying to measure up to a fleeting beauty ideal. I've tanned and starved and bought and primped in search of feeling beautiful, and none of it did anything to make me feel more so. In fact, based on my experience, it just made matters worse. But here's the good news: Because of all that useless chasing, I now have a whole slew of tips to help you feel pretty awful about yourself. Yep, you read that right. I have ten simple steps to help you feel your worst. These are tried-and-true methods, authenticated by me and the experiences of all womankind. I'm excited to introduce them to you, though I have a feeling you might already be acquainted.

God, thank You for making me a girl. I guess I should thank You for making girls, period! You didn't have to, and I see now that my female genes are a true creative masterpiece. I acknowledge that You made me the way I am *on purpose*. Teach me to see that as a good thing. Teach me how to recognize and enjoy the beauty You've woven into my DNA, even on the days when it's really hard to believe it. I love You, and I want to honor You by recognizing Your creative talent! Amen.

Discussion Questions

1. *Name five ways God created Eve to be different from Adam.*

    a.

    b.

    c.

    d.

    e.

2. *How are we beautiful just by being female?*

3. *Do you know any girls who are truly beautiful but can't see it? How does their blindness make you feel?*

    Is there any chance you are one of those girls?

4. *If I asked you the same questions I asked Cassidy, how would you answer?*

Q: *True or False: I believe I am beautiful inside and out.*
A:

Q: *On a scale of 1 to 10, how happy are you with the way you look?*
A:

Q: *True or False: If it had been up to me, I would have made me just the way I am.*
A:

Q: *What would you need to change in order to feel completely content with your body?*
A:

5. *What do you think keeps you from recognizing your true beauty? Jot down some thoughts on this in your journal.*

6. *Do you agree that "the more we focus on becoming physically beautiful, the uglier we feel"? Why or why not?*

Believe What You See On Screen

DIRECTIONS: Believe that the images you see every day in the media are 100 percent authentic. Assume those girls were born naturally uber-skinny and wake up every day with perfect hair, skin, and teeth. Then believe it's humanly possible for *you* to look like *that* in real life. Whatever you do, don't look into the pre- and post-production processes, where designers sell products by creating fake people.

Little known fact: I started my college career as a film production major. I even worked as an extra in Hollywood to make some cash. Although my experiences on set completely ruined the illusion of Hollywood glamour for me (think looong days and creepy coworkers), I did get to wear some pretty awesome costumes as a 70s hippie, sock-hop sweetie, blushing bride, and computer geek. I even got to throw pillows in a music video for a former Spice Girl. I'm pretty sure that will come back to haunt me someday.

If *you've* ever wanted to dabble in the movie industry, here's your chance. I want you to pretend you're the casting director for the next blockbuster, a film about a beautiful twentysomething girl who wins the heart of an unsuspecting-but-handsome hero. (Obviously, the plot isn't a big stretch. I think Hollywood has made three dozen such films this week alone.) Okay. So go ahead and pick out your hottie hero from today's lineup of your favorite actors. I'll wait.

```
LEADING MALE ROLE
Name:
```

Now for the starlet. You get to do what every casting director wishes they could do: create her from scratch. I want you to picture what you think she should look like and then fill out her "one sheet" below.

```
LEADING FEMALE ROLE
Name: "The Perfect Girl"
Height:
Dress size:
Bust-waist-hip measurements:
Eye color:
Skin color and texture:
Facial features (nose,
lips, and cheekbones):
Hair color and length:
```

I have a sneaking suspicion that your completely made-up leading lady is strangely (like freakily) similar to that of every other girl who reads this book, from her perfectly tanned, smooth skin to her cute button nose.

Sound fishy to you?

It shouldn't surprise us though. I'm going to venture to say the media plays a major role in creating the picture of perfection burned into our brains. (Yes, that could possibly be the biggest understatement in this entire book.) I just flipped through *Seventeen* magazine[1] and found 342 pictures of girls that fit part or all of the stats you probably wrote down on your one sheet: long legs; blue or green eyes; smooth, shiny hair; perfectly straight, white teeth; tan, smooth, shiny skin; and a size zero to four. That's a lot of pictures. But to give you even more perspective, the entire magazine is only 162 pages long! For just $2.99, I can buy a manual for how to look, think, and act to be considered beautiful by the world at large. A small price to pay for the girl intent on looking her best, eh?

Ad It Up

Pretty soon the endangered species list might include "blank spaces." Some sources say the average person sees up to five thousand ads a day.[2] Is that humanly possible? That's like twelve ads a second the entire seventeen hours you're awake! Companies have to come up with creative ways to get their products to stand out in a sea of stuff, so there are ads on subway turnstiles, on the sides of buildings, and in doctors' examination rooms. The CBS network even stamped ads for their TV shows on eggs—of the chicken variety—sold at grocery stores. Like I want to see "CBS Mondays: Leave the Yolks to Us" while making my spinach and mushroom omelet? Clever, but *no*. You might even see ads on the motion-sickness bags in the seat-back pocket on your next flight.[3] Can you imagine the logic? When I'm nauseated and about to hurl, am I really going to think, *What do we have here? A Subway ad, huh? I'll be sure to buy a sandwich when I land, right after I puke my guts out into the bag stamped with their subtle marketing campaign.*

Yeah, ads are everywhere. With so much competition, how's a chap supposed to make a buck? Advertisers know the only way to get people's attention is to be everywhere they look. Well that, or they can use the "secret weapon."

What is this secret weapon? you might ask. It's an advertising tool so powerful it can make both men and women take a second look at an ad selling everything from perfume to pet food. The secret weapon in advertising is—are you ready for it?—*a beautiful woman*. A picture of a woman draws people toward an ad like moths to a streetlight. Like shoppers to a semi-annual event. Like a PMS-ing gal to a pint of luscious, raspberry chocolate-chip gelato (not that I'd know anything about that). Advertisers know the draw of beauty. So they plaster images of gorgeousness on their ads to make men desire and women admire. They don't care whether the images are "realistic" or harm your body image. They're just looking to sell their product. And make money. And take lavish vacations in the Riviera.

I don't know what percentage of ads sport a beautiful woman, but I do know that in almost every single one of them, the woman pictured fits a very narrow description of beauty. Our casting experiment is proof. I also know that this narrow description of beauty has been created by our culture (we're going to explore that more in the next chapter). By "culture," I mean media, because in today's world, the media has a big role in forming our culture.

But is this image of "beauty" in your mind—the impression left by millions of ads and movies you've seen over your lifetime—for real? Does it even exist in the real world? That's what I set out to learn (play Sherlock Holmes theme music).

Myth Busters

"I have never yet seen, and you probably never will see, a fashion or beauty picture that hasn't been retouched."[4]

DEREK HUDSON, professional photographer

It all started in the 1930s, when photographers used lighting and soft focus to glamorize movie stars in print. A lot of makeup and some sultry dresses were all they needed to turn pretty women into beauty icons. That was then. This is now: In the twenty-first century, photographers use computer programs to completely alter everything about a woman. They create *fake people*.

I remember hearing as a teen that the photos I saw in ads and on magazine covers had been touched up. The news gave me some comfort when I looked in the mirror on prom night—decked out in a beautiful dress, perfect makeup, and professionally styled hair—and *still* didn't look like the picture I saw in *Teen Vogue*. But I had no idea just how much touching up "touching up" meant until I saw a video that transformed a normal girl into a Photoshopped beauty right before my eyes. I thought "touched up" meant they erased some pimples and gave a touch of tan. Oh no. In just over a minute of time-lapse video, stylists applied makeup, straightened and curled her hair, and then used photo-editing software to make her lips plumper, eyes bigger, eyebrows thinner and more arched, neck longer, forehead taller, face slimmer, and hair longer. The final "product" was then plastered to a billboard to underscore the fact that what we see in ads is nothing more than a computer-generated work of art.[5]

The process of taking a photographer's digital photo and making it print worthy is called post-work. Using photo-editing software, post-work designers can:

- Improve the light, color, and contrast of the picture.
- Magically transform the model's skin into blemish-free, silken, android-looking perfection. (Look, Mom—no pores!)
- Reshape her curves, waist, and bust. We're talking about adding or shaving *inches* from the model's hips, stomach, legs, and ta-tas.

- Make her grow taller or lengthen only certain features, such as her neck or legs.
- Make the color of her eyes more intense or just change the color altogether.
- Restyle, recolor, and texturize her hair.
- Change the background of the photo so it looks as though the model is somewhere else entirely.

Who needs beauty products when you have Photoshop? It's a one-stop shop for eyeliner, eye shadow, mascara, eyebrow filler, eye whitener, colored contacts, lipstick, concealer, foundation, skin contourer, pore minimizer, hair dye, plastic surgery, liposuction, and DNA manipulation.

Most of the women we envy in the photos we see aren't real. And if they're not real, then hoping to look like them is an exercise in stupidity! It's like looking at Monet's famous painting *Water Lilies* and then trying to become a lily pad. We can't become art.

I, like you, am glad girls are starting to see the truth: that most women in the media aren't all they're advertised to be. Most girls—85 percent, last I checked—at least know that the images they see have been altered.[6] That's a good place to start. I'm trying to do my part to get the news to the other 15 percent!

Here's the crazy thing: You'd think that if we knew we were looking at fake images, we wouldn't compare ourselves to them. That would make sense, right? But as you and I both know, girls can be completely irrational when it comes to beauty, and sound reason doesn't always make a dent in our envy! Knowing an image is "altered" doesn't erase the negative impact it can have on our view of our bodies. In the same study I mentioned, more than 30 percent of girls who knew better still said they were "unconfident to extremely unconfident about their body," even though one in three girls said they didn't think it was possible for them to have the body they aspired to have.[7]

These studies aren't news to us, though, are they? In our experience as girls, they make perfect sense. We know about Photoshop; some of us even use it ourselves. Yet we still struggle with body image (maybe more than at any other time in history). That's dangerous. *Really* dangerous. Let's talk about why.

Danger in Our Myth

The phony images advertisers try to pass off as fact aren't as harmless as they'd like us to believe. Obviously. But have you ever wondered who's *really* behind all this deception? Is it the advertisers? The models? The products? Who's to blame?

I'll give you a ~~little~~ big hint:

[The Devil] was a murderer from the beginning.
He has always hated the truth, because there is no
truth in him. When he lies, it is consistent with his
character; for he is a liar and the father of lies.
JOHN 8:44

When I think about the lies that Satan feeds us girls, my blood starts to boil. When I picture him filling the world with lies that prey on girls like you . . . argh! I'm starting to get all fired up just thinking about it! Because this is what he does, sis: He ever so subtly tells us that because we don't look like an image that doesn't even stinking *exist* in real life, we're not beautiful. We're not worth much. We don't deserve to hold our heads high with dignity. Satan's words are a direct contradiction to what God says about us, so when we choose to believe Satan's lies, he essentially gets us to tell God, "Why did You make me this way? What were You *thinking*?"

I'm not saying everyone who works in media or advertising is evil. Goodness, my own husband is a graphic artist! But I *am* saying that there is a very real spiritual battle going on, and Satan is using mankind's desire to get rich (through advertising) as a weapon against us. Ephesians 6:12-13 talks about the battle we fight:

> We are not fighting against flesh-and-blood enemies, but against evil rulers and authorities of the unseen world, against mighty powers in this dark world, and against evil spirits in the heavenly places.
>
> Therefore, put on every piece of God's armor so you will be able to resist the enemy in the time of evil. Then after the battle you will still be standing firm.

We're facing a serious enemy. Satan is not out for prisoners; he's out to kill us spiritually. And he knows that if he can get us to doubt what God has said, we're doomed. That's what happened in the Garden of Eden, you know. The dialogue went something like this (you can find the real convo in Genesis 3:1-5):

> **Satan:** Did God really tell you not to eat from any tree in the garden? Hmmm?
> **Eve:** Well, no, not exactly. We can eat from most of the trees here. God told us to stay away from only the tree in the middle of the garden. That one is definitely off-limits. God said not to even touch it or we'll die.
> **Satan:** *Die?* Come on, you don't really believe that, do you? God told you not to eat it because He knows that the moment you do, you'll see what's really going on. You'll be just like God, knowing everything, from good all the way to evil.

Did you notice how Satan twisted God's words? Well, it worked. Eve was swept away by the Devil's smooth-talkin' mumbo jumbo, and she disobeyed God. You know the rest of the story. We're all still under the curse of sin because of what went down in the Garden that day. And Satan is still manipulating truth to get us to turn our backs on God. In the realm of beauty, that crafty son of a snake is a master at twisting the truth that God's daughters are beautiful— inside *and* out—until we're confused with his lies and begin to doubt God. A modern-day garden dialogue might go something like this:

Satan: God didn't *really* say that you're beautiful just the way you are, did He? Come on—look at how this girl's body is perfectly proportioned, her blemish-free skin polished golden, her face the portrait of beauty. You don't really think you're as beautiful as *she* is, do you?

Eve: Well, no, I guess not. I certainly don't look like her, do I? Maybe God was just trying to make me feel better when He said that I'm beautiful.

Satan: That's right! He just didn't want you to feel jealous of other girls, so He told you all sorts of nice things to make you feel better about yourself. But if you *do* want to be beautiful—*really* beautiful—well, I can show you how. All you have to do is . . .

And so we run ourselves into the ground trying to look like the phony picture of beauty we see all around us. And in the end, what do we have to show for it? Nada. Unless you count a mangled, depressed heart and an empty wallet.

But why would Satan spend so much of his energy on this battle? What does he hope to gain by getting us to doubt our beauty and worth?

As girls, we want to be desirable, remember? If we don't feel that we measure up, we're much more likely to try to fill that hole in our hearts with anything *other* than God: an unhealthy relationship with a guy, acceptance from the wrong crowd, rebellion, or even success. But there's even more to the danger.

When we look in the mirror, if we're quick to point out all the things we would have done differently if *we* had been in charge of the DNA design process, it's like a slap in our Creator's face. We already touched on the fact that criticizing our bodies is equivalent to accusing God of making a mistake (or, for some of us, a *lot* of mistakes). You can probably see how that could create some tension in your relationship with God. Isaiah 45:9 warns us,

> What sorrow awaits those who argue with their Creator.
>> Does a clay pot argue with its maker?
> Does the clay dispute with the one who shapes it,
>> saying,
>> "Stop, you're doing it wrong!"

When Satan convinces us that God messed up when He was putting together our bodies, "sorrow awaits"—sorrow, like of the complete *misery* variety.

John 8:44 tells us that Satan can't stand the truth because there isn't a shred of truth in him. He hates the fact that you are uniquely and exquisitely beautiful, because he hates God and everything good that God creates. He'll do everything he can to pull you down. So when Satan comes around with his familiar accusations, tell him you're the *real* deal.

The Real Deal

Have you ever wondered why we call the girls on magazine covers models? I have. (But then, you'll find I tend to question everything.) I mean, think about the actual definition for a moment:

> model (^{1}mä-dəl), n.: an organism whose appearance
> a mimic imitates.[8]

A model is something that has reached perfection, something we want to be just like. We have model students, model citizens, and role models. But in the world of beauty and fashion, we have *super*models for that. Go figure.

Looking at Webster's definition, a model is something a mimic imitates. A mimic is someone who can't come up with anything original on her own. An imitator. A copycat. A poser. Those don't sound like favorable attributes to me, yet that's what we (myself included) become when we idolize beauty icons. Of course, when I take a step back and think about it logically, I'd rather be known as a girl with confidence, dignity, and unique beauty than Gisele's mini-me. (Most days, anyway. Just keeping it real.) The hard part is thinking about it logically when those fake images of perfection are shoved in my face at every turn. So what's a girl to do?

If you want to feel ugly, by all means, believe everything you see. But if you want to understand the *real* beauty you possess, it's time to quit idolizing cookie-cutter images and start imitating Someone else:

> Imitate God, therefore, in everything you do,
> because you are his dear children. Live a life filled

with love, following the example of Christ. He loved us and offered himself as a sacrifice for us, a pleasing aroma to God.

EPHESIANS 5:1-2

Imitate God. How? By living a life of love, just like our ultimate model, Jesus. I don't think our Savior was too preoccupied about His looks (see Isaiah 53:2; Matthew 6:28-29). He was too busy loving others to care if His muscles looked like the cover of *GQ* magazine. I don't want to spoil some good stuff to come, so for now, let me just say that when we spend our lives loving others instead of preoccupied with our looks, some really amazing things happen! And as the icing on the cake, when we follow Jesus Christ's example, we too can be a "pleasing aroma" to God—a fragrance better than any Chanel perfume.

So the next time you're tempted to throw a pity party because you don't have long-enough legs or a thin-enough waist or smooth-enough skin, take a step back and remember truth. If God wanted us all to look like cloned Barbie dolls, He could easily have gone that route. He can do that sort of thing—He's God! But the fact that He created so many versions of beautiful shows off His flair for the unique. For diversity.

Think about the variety of women God has made to fill this bright, big world! Since creating Eve, God has designed billions of women of every size and shape imaginable. Women with gorgeous dark skin and shiny black hair. Women with round butts and big ta-tas. Women with freckles and wrinkles and bulges and curves. Women with wide faces and narrow hips. Women with curly hair and dimples and moles and, yes, cellulite. He created us all with the same intent: to be beautiful. Different, and beautiful.

Oh yeah, and *real*.

God, You are a creative genius! You made beauty out of a bone, for crying out loud![9] Forgive me for doubting that You've made me beautiful too. It's just so hard, God, to remember and appreciate the beauty You've designed in me when I see so many images of exaggerated beauty all over the place. Help me remember the truth daily. I want to imitate You, God—not the fashion industry—as I follow Jesus' example of genuine love. Amen.

Discussion Questions

1. *What is an advertiser's "secret weapon"? Why does it get both men and women to look longer at an ad?*

2. *If you have a magazine handy, take a few minutes to browse through some pictures in ads while you play undercover Photoshop detective. What evidence do you see that the picture has been touched up? (Hints: look for hair or pores on the models' skin, unnatural hair color or texture, extra long or thin bodies, and so on.)*

3. *Do advertisers' visual tricks work? Do they make you want the products they're selling? What effects do their visual tricks have on your view of your body?*

4. *Why does Satan want you to doubt your beauty and worth? What would he accomplish if he got you to do that?*

5. *Think about one woman (of any age) you find beautiful but who doesn't necessarily look just like a supermodel. What makes her beautiful?*

6. *How could you encourage your friends to see their unique beauty too?*

7. *Take another look at Ephesians 5:1-2. What are three ways you can "imitate God" in the way you view beauty? Write your ideas in your journal.*

Get "The Look" at All Costs

DIRECTIONS: Because the images you see are obviously real, try to look just like them. Whatever your culture thinks is "hot" and "perfect," get that look at all costs. *All* costs. If you have money, spend it. If you have time, use it. If you've got a great body, flaunt it. Then take pictures of your look and share them on every social networking site you can think of. Pour everything you have and are into making others believe you're beautiful.

Isn't it funny how cultures worldwide define beauty in different ways? I recently saw a story about a woman named Panya who went to extreme lengths to become her home country's version of pretty. In Thailand, beauty happens to mean having light skin. Hard to believe for all us sun lovers out there who consider a golden tan the best accessory! But in Thailand, historically, having dark skin meant you worked in the rice paddies, so it was looked down on as low class. Still is. Because God gave Thai people gorgeous caramel-colored skin, Panya did what many Thai women do: She bought a jar of skin-lightening cream from the local open-air market and got to work creating "perfect."

At first the cream seemed to work like a charm. Panya was beyond excited, and she felt more confident and beautiful in her career as a singer. But one day she paid a price for beauty. She went out in the sun, and the bleaching agents in the cream burned her skin so badly that it started peeling off. She has never been the same since. Her skin is a blotchy mix of dark and light where her face and hands are permanently scarred. But the greatest damage wasn't to her skin; it was to her heart. Panya's husband left her, she lost her career as a singer, and she's embarrassed to go out in public.[1]

In the beginning of this book, we talked about a deep desire we girls have to be beautiful. That longing isn't bad: God gave it to us, after all! But when we're ruled by that desire, beauty becomes an idol. And we girls have been known to do some pretty crazy, stupid stuff to become "fairest of them all."

In a Beautiful World

Have you ever stopped to think about some of the lengths we go to for the sake of beauty? I've done a lot of looking into this over the years, and I've discovered some downright— I think *bizarre* pretty much covers it—things women have done over the course of history to be beautiful. Some of them make me wonder if we girls should be locked up for insanity! Here's just a sampling.

- Medieval women swallowed arsenic (a poison) to make their skin appear lighter. (Of course it was lighter—they were half-dead!) They also dabbed bats' blood on their faces to help their complexions. (Um, sick?)[2]

- Victorian women used extremely tight corsets and girdles to get a wasp waist (a waist so skinny it made the women look as though their bodies were segmented, like a wasp). We're talking waists of sixteen to eighteen inches on otherwise-curvy women.[3]

- Because small feet were considered beautiful in China for more than a thousand years, many parents broke and then bound their daughters' feet so they would stay small. The ideal size tootsie? Three inches! It was a painful and dangerous process, and women with bound feet walked slowly and deliberately (sadly, also considered beautiful).[4]

- To create their signature white faces, Japanese geishas plastered their faces with a paint made from—wait for it—nightingale poop. The geishas lived by countless rules, including a ban against falling in love.[5] Talk about a high price for beauty!

I wish I could say that girls have wised up as history has ticked on. I wish I could comfort us all by saying those extreme lengths women go to in order to be considered more beautiful are a thing of the past. But we haven't stopped chasing beauty, have we? Ladies all over the world go to pretty outrageous lengths to fit their societies' ideals of beauty and fashion. Here are just a few modern-day examples of what's considered beautiful around the world:

Uganda

In Uganda, the Hima (pronounced "heema") tribe thinks fat is beautiful. Yes, you heard that right. In fact, the more a woman resembles a man's cows, the better. No joke. Before a woman gets married, she spends two months in a "fattening hut," where she drinks more than five thousand calories a day of fresh milk and herbs to plump up as much as she can before her wedding day. She leaves the hut only to use the bathroom. But she needn't worry: In return for her sacrifice, she can easily add eighty pounds to her once-thin frame.[6] Oh, joy!

Thailand

Members of the Padaung sect of the Karen tribe in Thailand think long necks are a sign of beauty and wealth and will attract a better husband, so naturally, they doll up with a stack of heavy golden rings around their necks. Why not? They never take them off—not even to shower. The rings weigh as much as twenty pounds, and if they ever removed them, they'd have to spend their lives lying down because of the atrophy of their neck muscles.[7]

Asia

Western ideas of beauty have had a big impact in such countries as Japan and South Korea, where a woman's eyes are naturally almond shaped. To look more like the "doll-eyed" celebrities they see in the media, many Asian girls undergo a cosmetic surgery called the "double eyelid," where doctors cut the outer ends of their eyes to make them rounder and wider.[8]

My jaw drops every time I read about another strange definition of beauty from different corners of the world. I'm tempted to call those women desperate or strange or maybe a little crazy. But one look at my own culture—the good ol' USA—and I can't deny the truth: We are just as famous (if not more so) for chasing the illusive beauty ideal. We operate the same way as women across oceans and through the ages.

We mess with God's design in an effort to become what we think others will find most attractive.

Think about it. In America we yank our teeth around with metal brackets and wires to make them straighter and then soak them in toxic solutions to make them whiter. We stick little plastic discs in our eyes to change their color and permanently dye our skin with a needle and ink. We pay— *pay!*—for doctors to cut us open so they can remove fat in some places and enlarge us in others. We have Botox and Alli, push-up bras and Spanx. Yep, we are famous for getting the look at all costs.

I have been guilty as charged. I've baked my skin under the sun (slathered in baby oil, no less) to change my skin color. I've even done time in that giant radiation machine also known as a tanning bed. I've yanked off hair with gooey globs of wax (*Pain? What pain?*). I've dyed my hair with chemicals that would kill small rodents. I've applied tar to my eyelashes and put six holes in my body. I've spent money on clothes I didn't need. I've tried diet pills and battled an eating disorder to lose weight. Every day I wear a contraption made of wire, foam, and fabric that hoists and shapes my girls so they look perkier. The list is long, sister.

International beauty customs aren't sounding so strange anymore, are they?

Americans spend more than thirty *billion* dollars every year on makeup and beauty products.[9] As a society, we are certainly no different from the world at large, even though we're modern, educated young women who have supposedly been "liberated" from others' expectations. We still want to be beautiful—which isn't bad, remember. I'm not saying you shouldn't wear a bra, get braces, or buy that cute sundress you've been eyeing. But I do want you to question *why* you do the things you do. *I want you to be smart about your quest for beauty.* When we stop recognizing our natural gorgeousness and start trying to look like someone or something we're not, we'll always pay a price for beauty. It's up to you to look at your personal beauty equation and decide whether those costs are worth the benefit.

The Real Cost of Beauty

In the poorest areas of Rio de Janeiro, the *favelas* (slums), you'll still see a beauty salon on nearly every corner. The people there barely have any money, but the women in the *favelas* still feel a ton of pressure to look a certain way. One single mother gets her hair, eyebrows, and nails done every month. Local plastic surgeons give the locals discounts on procedures (how nice of them), so she saved up to have one done. In the end, she had to choose between getting breast implants or buying a better place for her and her daughter to live. Guess which she chose? The surgery.[10]

Sound dramatic? From where I sit, choosing better digs for my daughter over bigger breasts is a no-brainer. And while I could easily say that I'd never let beauty take over my better judgment, I know better. See, just last night I nearly laid down hundreds of dollars on an a-DOR-able and super-flattering genuine-leather jacket. (Can I mention how cute those brass zippers were or how beautiful I felt in all that tan-leather love?) In fact, the only reason I'm not living with buyer's remorse today is because I asked my sensible hubby for his opinion first. He said I was crazy. He was right! I had to plead temporary insanity caused by the lure of looking cute. I still can't believe Miss Penny-Pincher me was one credit-card swipe away from blowing my entire year's clothing budget! That's the allure of beauty.

It's always easier to judge others. But Jesus told us to take a good, long look at our own lives before we start pointing out others' sin (see Matthew 7:1-5). So let's take a look in the mirror for a sec. What are the costs of beauty you and I might charge to our accounts? Are they worth it?

Time

The average teen spends seven and a half hours a week getting ready.[11] Let's say that if we cut down our morning routines to the basics—brush teeth, quick shower, get dressed, brush hair—we could get by with spending only fifteen minutes a day on hygiene. By cutting out all the beauty stuff—makeup, hair straightening or curling, deliberating forever over which outfit to choose—we'd save 5.75 hours a week. Think of what you could do with that time! With 5.75 extra hours a week (quick math: 12.5 full days a year), you could fly to the moon and back. Twice.[12] Or you could read all six of Jane Austen's novels. You could have a shot at winning the Nobel Peace Prize, for crying out loud!

In all seriousness, one of the most common reasons girls give for not being able to spend time reading their Bibles is "no time." One thing's for sure: Spend less time on perfecting *your* beauty and you'll have more time to enjoy *God's*.

But let's be real: This doesn't have to be all or nothing. I'll be the first to tell you that I find some costs of beauty well worth my time! Yes, I could give up my *entire* beauty routine to have X more minutes with the Lord each day, but I don't. I still have makeup in my bathroom cabinet and a razor in my shower. To spend more time with the Lord, I *have* given up parts of my morning routine though, such as blow-drying and curling my hair most days, painting my nails, and shaving above my knees in the winter.

You have to find the balance that's right for you. Maybe

you could shorten a lengthy hairstyle or makeup routine or spend less time reading articles about beauty and fashion. Maybe you could pick out your clothes at night to save a few minutes the next morning or quit shaving your forearms or waxing your eyebrows. Just some ideas to get you thinking. Every minute you spend trying to look beautiful costs something, and you have to decide just how much you want to invest in your looks.

Money

Speaking of investing, did you know that the average woman spends $125,000 on clothes in her lifetime?[13] Or that she dishes out about $15,000 on makeup alone?[14] That's not even counting haircuts, colors, blowouts, lotions, perfumes, and piercings. If we add all those products and procedures to the mix, the verdict is shocking: We can easily spend thousands of dollars a year on looking pretty.

Is it worth it?

I'm going to let you in on a little secret: The beauty industry rakes in more than $400 billion dollars a year worldwide from women who don't feel beautiful enough.[15] Do you think the CEOs of those companies care about your happiness? Not so much. In fact, they want you to buy their products so badly, they'll do whatever they can to convince you that you can't be happy unless you buy their goods.

With that in mind, take a minute to think about anything you've bought (or your parents have bought for you) in the past year in the name of beauty. Peek in your closet, bathroom, jewelry box, and drawers. Do you have more clothes than you need? Half-used hair products collecting dust in the back corners of your cabinets? Purses or accessories you don't use because they're not "in" anymore? Most of us do. In fact, I didn't realize just how much I spent on stuff I really didn't need until I gave up clothes shopping for an entire year. I know—crazy! But guess what? I didn't go naked. My "fast" from shopping revealed just how easily I had bought the lie that I would be happier if I had the latest look. Ironically, I found way more happiness when I was content with what I already had. And the really cool part is that I was able to sponsor a little girl in South Africa with the money I saved that year—money that would have been spent filling my closet and shoe rack with more stuff that would have been out of style by Tuesday.

So, back to you. What is the cost, in dollars, of your beauty? Is that investment worth it to you, or would that money be better spent elsewhere?

Dignity

Giving up our dignity is a cost of beauty we don't think about much. In our culture, beauty equals sexiness. Just ask Victoria (who, ironically, makes big bucks by revealing Secrets). From magazines to the big screen, from social media to the pictures you pass on your way to school, the message is clear: The more of your body you show, the more beautiful you are. Not only is it a lie, but that kind of beauty also comes at another high cost.

Most girls would say they want guys to respect them for who they are, not just how they look. But when we dress "sexy" (showing off our womanly features, if you know what I mean), we send more messages than "I am beautiful." We also say such things as, "You don't have to work for my body; it's up for grabs" and "You can have me if you want me." As a girl myself, I know that's probably not what you're *trying* to say, but that's kind of how a guy's mind works. Although you might try to get "the look" because you want to be seen as beautiful, he might see that look as an invitation to look at places you probably don't want him gazing. We're going to talk a bit more about that later, but for now, let me give you this teaser: If you want to be *truly* beautiful, be "clothed with strength and dignity" (Proverbs 31:25). You'll find no hidden costs in that kind of beauty.

Beautiful Advice

Let's cut to the chase: Getting the look at all costs isn't worth the price we'll pay. Pouring everything we have and are into making others believe we're beautiful is pointless. Why? Because you and I can never reach "perfect beauty." There's only one perfect beauty: God Himself. The beauty you and I have is simply an imperfect reflection—just a taste—of Him as daughters made in His image.

We can understand our true beauty only when we recognize *God's* beauty and really know and believe what He says about us. As you draw closer to Him, He will show you just how exquisite you are! But there are also some steps you can take today to open your eyes to the truth that you are, in fact, beautiful. With that in mind, I'm going to share four tips that have completely changed my view of my own beauty and helped me see that in God's eyes, I already measure up.

1. Unplug from the drug.

I love apple fritters. They bring back memories of hitting the local doughnut shop after church as a kid. There's just something about those tender chunks of apple wrapped in fried dough and dipped in icing that is quite irresistible. The only problem is that every time I eat one, I get a serious stomachache. (Could it be the twenty-seven grams of sugar doused in enough fat to grease an engine? Hmmm.) I have a robust knowledge that apple fritters are terrible—even harmful—to my body, but if I give in and eat one, I'm still going to suffer the consequences of feeling icky the rest of the day. *Knowing* the truth doesn't protect me from harm.

The same is true of our media diet. I know that all those images of "perfection" I see in the media aren't true to life. I know they promote self-worth issues. I can even teach others the dangers of trying to look just like those images. But as I've learned in researching and writing this book, knowing the danger won't protect me from it. Since I started writing this book, I've struggled with comparison, discontentment, and preoccupation with my looks more than I have in a *decade*. Why? Because I've been swallowing picture after picture, article after article of outward beauty fritters, and my heart is feeling the effects.

To give a modern paraphrase of some of Jesus' most famous words, if reading a fashion and beauty mag causes you to sin (by making you discontent with the body God gave you), take that puppy and line your trash can with it. It's better to lose the four bucks you spent on it than to lose your life to sin. Same with your favorite TV shows. It's better to stop watching and face the ridicule of your friends than to sin by questioning how God designed you. (See Matthew 5:29-30 for Jesus' actual words.)

If you want to be truly happy with who you are—not who you could be if you tried hard enough—then it might be time to unplug from the media drug. Even though we know they're fake, something in our brains still can't take the onslaught of images without blowing a confidence fuse. If you disconnect from the constant IV drip of images, you'll be amazed at the results.

2. Spend wisely.

The Bible is full of teachings about money. If we took all God's commands about cash and squished them into one simple truth, it would be this: All your money is really God's, so spend wisely. God has made you His manager, and He wants to see your receipts at the end of your life. He says that not to scare us (He is full of grace for our failings) but rather to help us keep money in perspective. The money God gives you is a tool. You can potentially use that tool to chase beauty or to get friends or to look cool or to make yourself happy. Or you can use it as a tool to build God's Kingdom: helping the poor, serving the outcasts, and spreading the Good News of the gospel.

When Jesus taught people not to worry about what they were going to eat or wear, He knew they would have to spend some of their money on those things. But He also knows just how easily we justify spending way more than we need to! That's why He said,

> Don't worry about [food or clothes]. . . . These things
> dominate the thoughts of unbelievers, but your
> heavenly Father already knows all your needs. Seek the
> Kingdom of God above all else, and live righteously,
> and he will give you everything you need.
> MATTHEW 6:31-33

God knows that His girls have a desire to be beautiful. He also knows that when we seek His Kingdom instead of our beauty, we'll find what we're really looking for—what we *really* need.

3. Celebrate natural.

The day I learned that our culture's focus on beauty is driven by marketing campaigns, I felt like Dorothy discovering that the Wizard of Oz was all smoke and mirrors. Since then, I've begun to question everything about my beauty routine. *Do I really need that product? Who says I have to wash my hair every day? Are potions in bottles really any better than natural alternatives?* Of course I've hung on to some routines, like shaving my legs. (My apologies to my beautiful Brazilian friends, but I just can't seem to let that one go!) But I've eliminated a ton of products over the past few years, from face wash to lotions to hair products, and haven't missed them one bit.

Natural rocks. It's often more effective, and almost always cheaper, than the packaged, marketed, name-brand stuff. And when we stop relying on products and trends to make us beautiful, we find that we're already more beautiful than we realized. Boys dig natural beauty. Girls dig natural beauty. God does too. (That's my guess anyway, since He made us "au naturel.")

If you want to join the natural conversation, meet me over at LifeLoveandGod.com and search for "Health & Beauty." We can share ideas and ditch unnecessary products together!

4. Be content.

I've saved the best for last. If you really want to know and feel just how beautiful you are, work on contentment. This is the great secret of life: Be okay with you and with what you have. First Timothy 6:6-7 says,

> True godliness with contentment is itself great wealth. After all, we brought nothing with us when we came into the world, and we can't take anything with us when we leave it.

We can't take anything with us—not our makeup, our hair straighteners, or those perfectly retouched photos we posted of ourselves online last week. We can't even take our bodies with us when we die! (Lucky for us, we'll get new bodies, fit for eternity; see 1 Corinthians 15:35-53.) And if we can't take any of it with us, why waste so much time, energy, and money on it today?

Here's another verse to ponder:

> We don't look at the troubles we can see now; rather, we fix our gaze on things that cannot be seen. For the things we see now will soon be gone, but the things we cannot see will last forever.
>
> 2 CORINTHIANS 4:18

Can you imagine how honored God would be if His daughters were actually content with how they looked and what they had? With all the crazy lengths that women have gone through, and still go through, all over the world to be considered beautiful, what if *we* were different? What if we put a limit on the amount of time and money we spent on beauty so that we could spend *ourselves* on more important things—Kingdom things?

I don't know about you, but I'm inspired to stop chasing false perfection and start living like the real deal! Will you pray for that with me?

> God, I know that beauty isn't a bad thing. You are Beauty itself, so I know it can't be! But I'm not sure what real beauty is versus what others have convinced me is beautiful. Please help me see the difference. I want to be truly beautiful— beautiful in Your eyes, God. And I want to be

content with that beauty because I'm sick of
chasing "perfection." I'm sick of trying to become
something I'm not. Help me be wise in how I
spend my time and money, what I watch, and
who I look up to. I love You, Daddy! Amen.

Discussion Questions

1. *Which of the worldwide beauty trends do you find
   funniest? Scariest? Most relatable?*

2. *Can you think of any ways you or your friends have tried to
   get "the look" that would sound crazy or funny to another
   part of the world?*

3. *What are your personal "costs of beauty"? Write them in
   your journal and evaluate them one at a time. For example, how much time and money do you spend each month
   on beauty? Do you think that's a fair amount, or do you
   need to cut back?*

4. When can dignity be a cost of beauty?

5. Why is it sometimes helpful to take a break from media—to "fast" from it?

6. If all our money is really God's, how much of it do you think He'd want us to spend on making ourselves look pretty?

7. How do companies get us to buy products we didn't know we "needed"?

8. How can 1 Timothy 6:6-7 help us keep our quest for beauty in perspective?

Compare Yourself
to Every Other Girl

DIRECTIONS: Compare yourself to everyone else. It doesn't matter if she has different DNA; you should be able to look just like her, so keep trying until you do. Let jealousy and pride destroy potentially great friendships. Just for good measure, keep your insecurities tied tight around you, like armor, so no one can hurt you.

We've talked a lot about envy and chasing the image of "perfection" we see in the media, but those girls we see on paper or on a screen aren't the only females we get jealous of, are they? Our friends, family members—even girls we pass on the street—can bring on many an insecurity!

Like most girls, I really struggled with this in high school and college. It didn't help that my college roommate was the spittin' image of an Abercrombie model. True story: She and I were walking in the mall one day when a talent scout flagged us down. He took one look at me and then asked *her* to come to a model search later that day. How about that for a little self-esteem boost? I learned a lot in our time rooming together, though. At the top of the list, I realized it was completely pointless to compare my body to hers. I couldn't expect to fit into her size itsy-bitsy pants any more than she could take my spot on the volleyball team. We were different. Both beautiful, but in different ways.

That took me a *long* time to figure out, mind you (all four years of college, to be exact-ish). For girls, comparing our looks just comes naturally.

Guys do not understand this. They play their own comparison games, sure, but contrasting their butts, hair, stomachs, legs, and fingernails with other guys doesn't top the list. Case in point: A few weeks ago, I went to an NBA game with some friends. During halftime, the cheer team came out as usual to "pump us up" (naturally by shaking their stuff). As they were twirling and twerking in their painted-on shorts and crop tops, my husband's best friend, Doug, leaned over to say something to me.

"So, what do girls think about that?" he asked, pointing at the dancers. "Because when I look around, the guys in the audience may or may not be watching, but the girls are *all* watching." Here he paused, then added, "Intently."

It was true. Just about every set of female eyes in the audience—including mine—was glued to the perfect little figures with pom-poms swirling around center court.

I knew the answer to Doug's question like I know the sky is blue, but just to be sure, I leaned over and repeated the question to the girl on my left. She confirmed my prognosis: "We're comparing," she said. "I mean, my hair could never look like that, even on my very best hair day." Then she and I tried to explain to Doug why we girls were torturing ourselves by inspecting every shapely curve and shiny limb shaking it down on center court. I don't think we made a lot of sense to Doug, but I'm guessing *you* know exactly what I'm talking about!

Why do we compare? I suspect it goes back to that longing we have to be considered beautiful. But it also comes from the plain ol' evil desires in our hearts. James (Jesus' brother) put it this way:

> What is causing the quarrels and fights among you? Don't they come from the evil desires at war within you? You want what you don't have, so you scheme and kill to get it. *You are jealous of what others have,* but you can't get it, so you fight and wage war to take it away from them.
>
> JAMES 4:1-2, EMPHASIS ADDED

Now, I don't see any literal wars being fought between girls over who has the best hair, but you can't deny that we can be downright catty and childish over this stuff sometimes. James was right: We compare because we're jealous. We're jealous because of the "evil desires at war within" us. None of it is pretty.

I don't think the question of why we compare is any less important than what happens when we compare. Most of us don't have any idea just how dangerous the comparison game is. Judging another girl's looks can feel as natural as breathing or blinking or putting on lip gloss. But just because something feels natural doesn't mean it's okay with God or safe for us. The truth is, the second we judge another girl's appearance, we invite one of two monsters to come out and play—and neither of them plays nice!

The Vain Monster: Pride

Did you know that Satan, God's archenemy, wasn't always evil? In fact, when God created him, He gave Lucifer (his real name) amazing beauty and even power. He was one of the good guys. So what happened to him?

> You [Lucifer] were the model of perfection,
> full of wisdom and exquisite in beauty.
> You were in Eden,
> the garden of God.
> Your clothing was adorned with every precious stone . . .
> all beautifully crafted for you
> and set in the finest gold.
> They were given to you
> on the day you were created.
> I ordained and anointed you
> as the mighty angelic guardian.
> You had access to the holy mountain of God
> and walked among the stones of fire.
> You were blameless in all you did
> from the day you were created
> until the day evil was found in you. . . .

So I banished you in disgrace
    from the mountain of God.
I expelled you, O mighty guardian,
    from your place among the stones of fire.
Your heart was filled with pride
    because of all your beauty.
Your wisdom was corrupted
    by your love of splendor.
So I threw you to the ground
    and exposed you to the curious gaze of kings.
EZEKIEL 28:12-17, EMPHASIS ADDED

What happened to Lucifer? Pride happened. He didn't want to be ordinary; he didn't want to be second to anybody. He looked at his own limited beauty, power, and influence as an angel, and then he looked at God, who was . . . well, *God*, and he just couldn't take it. He wouldn't stand for anything less than personal perfection. Because only God is perfect, Lucifer tanked.

Let's look at verse 17 again: "Your heart was filled with pride because of all your beauty." When we look at another girl and think, *I'm sure glad my [butt, arms, hair, skin, teeth, whatever] doesn't look like that,* we're in dangerous territory. We can't think less of someone's *outsides* without pride overtaking our *insides*. And when we start patting ourselves on the back because of how pretty we are, we're in the same danger of deceiving ourselves ("corrupting our wisdom") that Satan was.

So what's a girl—a girl prone to comparison—to do? Let's go back to James 4 to find some effective ammo against the Vain Monster:

[God] gives grace generously. As the Scriptures say,

> "God opposes the proud
> but *gives grace to the humble.*"

So humble yourselves before God. Resist the devil, and he will flee from you. . . .

Don't speak evil against each other, dear brothers and sisters. . . . God alone, who gave the law, is the Judge. . . . What right do you have to judge your neighbor?

JAMES 4:6-7, 11-12, EMPHASIS ADDED

That's good stuff, isn't it? We shouldn't speak—or even think—mean things about other girls because we have no right to! Thankfully, we can ask God to give us grace to stand against the temptation to boost our own egos by looking down on other girls in our lives. As we work on not judging others, simply loving them instead, humility opens our eyes to see *their* unique beauty too.

The Green Monster: Jealousy

Have you heard the phrase *green with envy*? When we compare our body with someone else's, the other monster that can attack is jealousy, and it is one fierce foe! James describes jealousy as "earthly, unspiritual, and demonic" (3:15) and says that where you find jealousy, you'll also find "disorder and evil of every kind" (verse 16). He's not messing around! Jealousy mangles our hearts. King Solomon saw just how badly envy can eat away at a person's heart. That's why he said, "A peaceful heart leads to a healthy body; jealousy is like cancer in the bones" (Proverbs 14:30).

Jealousy eats at us like *cancer*. If you've ever watched someone you love suffer and wither from that disease, you know just how strong a statement Solomon was making.

When we look at the girls around us and point out all the ways we like their bodies more than ours—when we want what we don't have and long for it with fierce passion—it eats away at us. It cripples us spiritually and emotionally, but Solomon wasn't just being poetic; our emotional health can show up in very real physical ways. (Have you ever gotten a cold sore during finals or come down with a bad cold when your family is going through a stressful time?) Jealousy can literally hurt us.

Not only is jealousy harmful, it's also just plain stupid. Why? Making jealousy a habit is like trying to live on a diet of iceberg lettuce and lemon juice: it tastes sour and offers zero nutrition! We feel like junk when we make the comparison, and then we continue to feel like junk because we're not getting the spiritual nutrition we need. When we think of it that way, envying other girls doesn't seem worth the negative effect it has on us, does it?

Slaying Your Monsters

So we know that God hates pride and that jealousy kills us like cancer, but how do we *stop* comparing ourselves to others when it comes so naturally (because we are sinful people)? That's not an easy question to answer, but 1 Peter 2:1-3 is a great place to start.

> Get rid of all evil behavior. Be done with . . .
> jealousy. . . . Like newborn babies, you must
> crave pure spiritual milk so that you will grow
> into a full experience of salvation. Cry out for
> this nourishment, now that you have had a taste
> of the Lord's kindness.

How do we ditch pride and jealousy? By changing our diet. Instead of the iceberg lettuce and lemon juice we've been choking down, we've got to feast on the "pure spiritual milk" God offers us (which is His Word, His ways, and His presence). Psalm 34:8 says, "Taste and see that the LORD is good. Oh, the joys of those who take refuge in him!"

Let me tell ya, when you "taste and see" just how good God is, you'll lose your appetite for measly lemon and lettuce! He gives such joy to those who turn to Him—to those who invest in their relationship with Him and consider Him in every corner of their lives. Pride and jealousy destroy us from the inside out, but God's milk does a body good.

I'm confident that as you get your fill of God's "spiritual milk" and begin to "grow up," you'll be less tempted to compare yourself to the girls around you. But I also have a few suggestions to help jump-start your contentment today. So let's get busy slaying some monsters, shall we?

Draw from your DNA.

Like I (finally) figured out about my college roommate, no two bodies are alike. Your height, hair texture, skin tone, cheekbones, nose, and general body shape have nothing to do with you or how hard you "try" and everything to do with the DNA God gave you. You could think of DNA as the recipe God used when He made you. You'll get further in your quest for contentment if you thank Him for it instead of fight against it!

How about a personal example? I've long been convinced God threw some flamingo genes into the mix when he made the women in my family. We have *loooong*, skinny legs and short, rounder torsos. True confession: I used to hate my midsection. Instead of just accepting the fact that I'll always have long legs and a short, roundish torso (because that's the way God made me . . . and my mom and my aunts), I was convinced I should look like my good friend Sara with her lean limbs *and* washboard stomach. Comparing my DNA to hers drove me crazy because, let's face it, what I wanted just wasn't going to happen. Even now, though I am at a good, healthy weight, my stomach just won't sport a six-pack like Sara's did. It's just not going to happen. And I'm over it now—mostly.

When we start looking at our DNA with thankfulness,

a really cool thing happens: We start to see the good in our "recipe." We start to see that God wasn't crazy when He designed us; He's just partial to variety. There are many kinds of beautiful, and your particular mix of chromosomes is one of them.

Prize your unique beauty.

Your DNA, combined with all the experiences of your life, make you unlike anyone else on the planet. Those airbrushed, nipped-and-tucked images lack the detail and character possessed by real-life, uniquely beautiful girls like you and me.

Ironically, we usually view the characteristics that make us different as ugly. Instead of seeing a sprinkling of freckles or an extra-wide smile as uniquely beautiful, we criticize and even despise our differentness. That's crazy! We've got to stop letting the media convince us that there's only one way to be beautiful. Sometimes our differences are the most beautiful things about us. Remember those flamingo legs? Yeah, well my husband is gaga over them. Ha! Who knew? And I want to help you pinpoint some of those different, beautiful things about you that maybe you're tempted to get mad at. But before we do that, I want to clarify something that's really important to understand:

Acknowledging your beauty isn't prideful.

God created your body, not you! You're just reminding yourself what a fabulous job He did. In fact, recognizing God's mad beauty-making skills can be a form of praise. You can worship Him by acknowledging that "body and soul, [you are] marvelously made!" (Psalm 139:14, MSG). So are you ready to say this with me?

I am beautiful.

That wasn't so hard, was it? Now we're going to take this a step further, because it's one thing to *say* you're uniquely beautiful and another thing to *believe* it. I want you to tell me exactly *why* you're beautiful. What's lovely or unique about you? In the following box, draw a picture of yourself on the right. (If you're not an artist, don't sweat it. As you can tell by my drawing, stick figures are my specialty!) Then, once you've drawn yourself, label five characteristics of your body that are uniquely beautiful. I've done it too, just to break the ice.

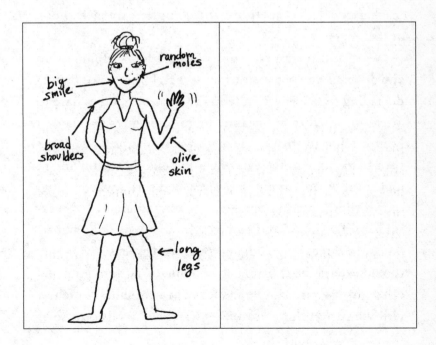

Look girls in the eyes.

My hope is that you'll get to a place where you can see another girl's beauty and admire it with pure motives, just like praising God for a beautiful sunset or a moving song. But if you're not there yet—if you can't seem to look at another girl without comparing yourself to her—I have one more piece of advice that can help you kick the comparison habit. If you want to kill the monsters of pride and jealousy stone-dead, focus on a girl's eyes when you're talking to her, and when you're not talking to her, if you can't resist the temptation to critique or envy her body, try not to look her way at all. This goes for friends, frenemies, sisters, mothers, teachers, clerks, competitors, and complete strangers. Look at their eyes.

We girls can get pretty upset at guys for scanning us up and down like an object, can't we? We feel (rightly so) that it's degrading to be viewed in terms of what our bodies have to offer—of whether we measure up to some guy's standard of beauty. I'll be the first to say that I want—I *expect*—a gentleman to look me in the eyes when I'm talking to him and to look away when I'm not. However (and this is where things start hitting close to home), are we any different? If I measure a girl's "assets" and compare my body to hers, aren't I doing the same thing: judging? But it makes sense that a lady should extend the courtesy of eye contact, both to guys and other girls. What a simple and loving way to show our fellow girls the respect they deserve.

The Beauty of a Smile

Remember Proverbs 14:30? It said that jealousy eats away at our hearts like cancer. It also gave us a positive by-product of *not* comparing: "A peaceful heart leads to a healthy body." We all want peace, don't we? And I can't think of anything that shows a peaceful heart like a smile.

Last week, my five-year-old daughter, Logan, unexpectedly reminded me of this. My little Feisty Spice had gotten in trouble for something and was sitting on her bed waiting for me to come talk to her about the consequences of her actions and all that. I sat next to her, all serious and mom-like, ready to dive into some lecture about sowing and reaping and yada yada. (One of the downsides of being my offspring is hearing endless lectures!) Anyway, she went and did something sly and silly that completely ruined my whole tough-guy approach and made me break into a big grin. Logan stopped, cocked her head to one side, and said in her adorable five-year-old voice, "Mommy, you're so pretty when you smile like that!"

Melted.

Her words had me thinking all week, and as I watched the women around me—at church, in the park, at a store—I noticed that Logan was right on: There's nothing as beautiful as a smile. A smile shows confidence, joy, and peace with yourself. A smile is contagious and brings life to the people around you.

And here's the thing: I can't compare and smile at the same time. Neither can you. Being preoccupied with that girl's hair and that other girl's behind and that *other* other girl's cheekbones—it's all-consuming! It's also heavy and exhausting, and it steals the peace right from our hearts.

"A peaceful heart"—a heart okay in its own skin—"leads to a healthy body." A content heart also leads to a lot of smiles (not to mention friends, joy, love, and opportunities). So unless you really do want to feel ugly, recognize and appreciate your own beauty and say good-bye to comparisons for your own good.

> Father, thank You for using a one-of-a-kind recipe when You created me. I'm sorry for not always appreciating the unique beauty You've given me, and I just want to take a minute to tell You I think You did a marvelous job. Forgive me for the times I've looked around at other girls You've made, trying to gauge my beauty based on theirs. That isn't right, and I'm sorry. Help me to kill any jealousy and pride in my life so I can have the "peaceful heart" Your Son Jesus died to give me. Amen.

Discussion Questions

1. *Most of us know that comparing our bodies to images in magazines isn't realistic, but is it okay to compare ourselves to "real" people? Can you think of any dangers we face when we compare our beauty to the girls around us?*

2. *Copy James 4:1-2 into your journal. According to those verses, why are we tempted to compare? What evil desires war within us?*

3. *What two monsters come out to play when we compare ourselves to others?*

4. *Which of the two monsters do you run into most often?*

5. *How can understanding and accepting your DNA help free you from jealousy? From pride?*

6. *Do you think it would be hard to look only at only another girl's eyes and not the rest of her body?*

7. *Why isn't it possible to smile and compare at the same time?*
    Which of the two has better rewards?

Believe Nasty Words
(Yours and Others')

DIRECTIONS: If people tell you you're the wrong size, shape, or color, believe them. Their opinions are far and away more trustworthy than those of the God of the universe, so don't bother learning or believing what God says about you. And if you ever start to feel even a little bit good about your body, tear yourself right back down to size with your own degrading words.

I remember the day clearly. I boarded school bus 11, thankful I had made it through another day of fifth grade. The unusually warm spring weather had me in shorts and a cheerful mood as I flopped down on a green pleather bench seat a few rows from the back of the bus. Some boy I didn't really know sat next to me and stuck his backpack under the seat. As the bus left the school yard for the hour-long drive home, I faced the window, watching trees, sagebrush, and an occasional cow pass by. I rested my feet just below the top of the seat in front of me, putting my bare legs at a forty-five-degree angle. It was my usual, haven't-got-a-care-in-the-world position. I was oblivious to the fact that the boy next to me was casting sideways glances at my bare legs, which were now at his eye level, gawking at something I had never really noticed before. Finally he asked in a snarky tone, "Why are your legs so hairy?"

Completely caught off guard, I shot back, "Why are you so stupid?"

I don't remember anything else about that bus ride home. What I do remember, though, is that the very next morning, I took my mom's white disposable razor from the top shelf in the shower and shaved my legs for the first time. In the span of six words, that boy took me from confident and unaware to insecure and embarrassed.

That's the power of words.

I wish my run-in with lame-boy was the only time I believed I were less beautiful because of someone's words. You and I both know that people can say way crueler things than that—things that scar us for life. In fact, many of our insecurities were born when someone said something unkind to us or about us. "Ski feet" and "big nose" were two phrases spoken to me nearly two decades ago that have never left my brain. It sounds silly to admit, but I have always been self-conscious about my nose because of those careless words spoken to me—just once—by someone I looked up to. Even the kind words that person said over the years didn't erase the permanent recording.

To make matters worse, the mean words other people say about us then become ammo for the enemy within. The evil word ninja inside our own heads can be the cruelest wordsmith of them all, can't she? She knows what words will cut the deepest, and she jumps at every opportunity to use them. If you listened to your own self-talk on any given day, would you hear words like these?

> *You're bigger than her. Fatty.*
> *Could your hair get any frizzier?*
> *You look like an Oompa Loompa.*
> *Maybe if you weren't as flat as a wall, he would notice you.*
> *You're not popular because your skin looks like the cratered surface of the moon.*

Whether the words that hurt you come from others or your own mind, I'm sure you've experienced that negative words have tremendous power! Before we talk about that power in more detail, I want you to take a few minutes to think about the specific words that have wounded you and the effects they've had on your view of yourself. Once you've done that, read on.

The Power of Words

"God said . . ."

And the rest is history.

Using His words, God created the entire universe (see Genesis 1). Everything we know in this life—from the food we eat to the laws of science to our favorite vacation spot— exists because He *said* it should. Is that mind-blowing or what? Obviously God's words carry more bang than ours do, with

His being God and all that. But because we're the only life-form on the planet created in His image, our words also carry power. He's left it up to us to decide whether we're going to use our words for good (as He does) or for evil (as Satan does). The book of Proverbs has a lot to say about the two choices.

Good Words . . .	Evil Words . . .
Are a life-giving fountain (10:11)	Conceal violent intentions (10:11)
Give helpful, wise advice (10:31-32)	Are deceptive and perverse (10:31-32)
Save lives (12:6)	Are like a murderous ambush (12:6)
Bring many benefits (12:14)	Make the speaker a fool (10:18)
Heal (12:18)	Cut down (12:18)
Are a tree of life (15:4)	Crush others' spirits (15:4)
Are like honey: sweet and nourishing (16:24)	Lead to strife and problems between friends (16:28)

It's no wonder James said, "A word out of your mouth may seem of no account, but it can accomplish nearly any-thing—or destroy it!" (James 3:5, MSG). Yeah, words have *that* much power.

When I read these verses, I'm reminded that I have a big responsibility to use my words carefully. Easier said than done, right? Is it just me, or is your tongue intent on living up to the nickname James gave his: "a restless evil" (James 3:8, HCSB)? Using my words to build up instead of tear down is a daily fight, a battle I'll wage my entire life! Others are fighting the same battle, and sometimes we become the target when their tongues win. What can we do when someone speaks words to us that cut to the heart?

First, we can admit that it hurts. "Sticks and stones may break my bones, but words will never hurt me" sounds nice and all, but there's nothing further from the truth. Cruel, careless words hurt just as bad as a swift kick to the shins—sometimes worse! But we also have to learn how not to let cruel words destroy us, because people are going to say stupid stuff they shouldn't say. It's a fact of life: "Not a single person on earth is always good and never sins" (Ecclesiastes 7:20). And if we let those words become our reality, if we replay those labels in our minds and define ourselves by them, we're hurting only ourselves.

In the next two verses of Ecclesiastes 7, Solomon gives a practical reason why we should stop listening to others' negative words: "Don't eavesdrop on others—you may hear your servant curse you. For you know how often you yourself have cursed others" (verses 21-22).

In other words, don't take other people's negative words to heart, because you know that you've said careless things too. Just like you probably weren't thinking clearly when you said them (you were probably acting out of emotion), the person who has wounded you with words is human too. Now, there are some people out there who know exactly what they're doing and wield their words like weapons on purpose. We're going to talk about how to deal with those people a little later. But first let's talk about how to get past the occasional, careless "evil words" that come from usually well-meaning people.

Who Do You Trust?

Whether people's hurtful words roll off your back or pierce your heart comes down to a simple question: Who do you trust more? Do you trust the words of the person who said those hurtful things about you (or do you trust *yourself*, if you're doing the name calling), or do you trust God's words? My friend Abby put it this way:

> A girl can feel only as valued as she respects the person who is valuing her. When a man or woman I trust and hold in high esteem sees me as beautiful and valuable, I begin to believe it more and more. Maybe if we understood how much God values and loves us—and how important His opinion is—it would change how we view ourselves.

It's true! I don't mean this to sound harsh, but would you feel more confident about your beauty if an unpopular, awkward guy said you looked pretty today or if you heard the exact same words from that cute guy you've been crushing on all year? Hands down, you'd feel giddy all over when the guy you admire complimented you, right?

How much you value someone dictates how much you'll value their words.

So let's take this another step. When a person puts you

down—guy, girl, young, old, popular, cruel—you'll take those words to heart only if you value that person more than you value God. That might sound extreme, but when you stop to think about it, it makes sense. If you're at a place in your relationship with God where you admire Him more than anyone else, other people's opinions won't matter as much as His. Even your own opinion won't matter as much! I didn't say that their words won't hurt, but they don't have to pierce your heart. They don't have to devastate you or define you. I know it's not easy to get to that place, and I know that in a fallen world, we can't completely ignore what other people say about us. But I do know that we can turn the tide of feeling worthless and ugly and start feeling like the beautiful, worthy girls we are when we know and believe what God has spoken about us.

So what has He said about you?

Love Letters

When you're head over heels about someone, you can't help but tell him. It brings you joy to express everything you notice, admire, and love about that person. My cowboy was no different. When we were dating and engaged, Paul showered me with pages and pages of the absolute sweetest words I had ever heard in my life. He wrote me e-mails, sent me letters, and even wrote songs that told me just how enraptured he was with me. (I know—spoiled doesn't begin to describe it!) He told me words like,

You shine. It's as if you radiate this certain type of magic, and anyone anywhere near you is touched by it.

You're beautiful. Not specific? Soft skin, gorgeous eyes, amazing smile, sexy legs, stomach to die for, shoulders of a woman, long fingers (I like that). Hair, arms, toes—I love everything about your body!

You're intelligent. You seek the truth and find it. You can figure stuff out and find errors in things. You are a perfect "sounding board" for my crazy ideas, and I can trust you with the deepest things I know.

You make me feel free. Truly free.

I doubt you'll be surprised to hear that I devoured his words. I journaled about what he said on the phone, memorized the lyrics to the songs he wrote me, and read his hundreds of letters and e-mails over and over (and over). I hung on his words. I prized them. I *believed* them.

Rereading his words was no sacrifice! I wanted to know what he thought of me and what dreams he had for us. I wanted to know that he saw me as beautiful. I wanted to know that he *loved* me. And when he actually said those words to me for the first time during a phone call while we were hundreds of miles apart . . . well, here's a peek into my journal so you can see what effect *that* had on me!

"Oh, have I told you yet?" he asked as we said good-bye on the phone last night. I answered that familiar question with a playful, "No, what?"

"I love you."

My heart stopped—I literally couldn't say a word. I could barely breathe for the pressing, swelling feeling in my whole body. His usual "you're beautiful" or "I miss you" would have made me smile and blush, but these words—these three unexpected, yet so welcome, words—literally turned my world upside down.

The power of words! What girl doesn't want to hear that she is beautiful and loved from someone she respects and adores?

Words from a suitor have the greatest power of all.

And this is what I really want you to see: You are being pursued by the greatest Prince of all time! Jesus, the Prince of Peace, calls us (the church) His bride. Jesus desires you, pursues you, adores you, and loves you enough to *die* for you. He moved heaven and earth to be near you! With a love for you like that, shouldn't you hang on His words, base your worth on them, and savor them like a bar of 72 percent cacao dark chocolate? Yep.

God has written you a love letter (the Bible), and He's not shy about saying how He feels about you. In its pages, He waxes eloquent about your beauty, purpose, gifts, and value. God tells you *who* you are and *whose* you are. And He explains what He's willing to do to be with you forever because He loves you *that* much! He says,[1]

> *You are My treasured possession.*
> Deuteronomy 7:6

> *I made your body beautiful and complex, and I did a masterful job!*
> Psalm 139:14

In My eyes, you are without fault.
You are perfect!
Ephesians 1:4

Even before I made the world, I loved
you and chose you to be Mine.
1 Thessalonians 1:4; Ephesians 1:4

You are a child of the light—My light.
Ephesians 5:8

You are a citizen of heaven; you
belong with Me.
Philippians 3:20

I have bought you back from death
and forgiven you for everything
you've ever done.
Ephesians 1:7

You are a beautiful, new creation!
2 Corinthians 5:17

Wow! He says so much more about you, but I don't want to give away all His sweet nothings at once. I pray you'll read the Bible for yourself and discover little by little just how much God adores you. His words give life, and they'll change how you view everything about yourself, including your beauty. As you savor and believe His words about you, insecurity will turn to confidence, and what others say about you won't matter so much. Value God, and you'll value what He says about you.

Putting a Stop to Attacks

But what about those words that cut *really* deep? What about verbal bullying, slamming, shaming, and shredding? That's called verbal abuse, and you don't need to put up with it. If it's in your power, put an end to the attacks. I know that's hard to do, especially if the person is going out of his or her way to be cruel (in person or online), but don't give up the fight. In this world, we will have "many trials and sorrows" (John 16:33), but that doesn't mean we have to take it when someone pelts us with vicious words over and over. I believe that God would want you to get help from others to stop verbal abuse, and I'd encourage you to reach out to a parent, teacher, or support group for help.

In Zephaniah 2:10, God comforted the Israelites by reminding them that He heard other nations' cruel words against them and would make sure the perpetrators met justice for their crimes. He said, "They will receive the wages of their pride, for they have scoffed at [made fun of] the people of the LORD of Heaven's Armies." And you don't want to mess with the Lord of Heaven's Armies! It's reassuring to know that even though mean words can hurt us, God knows, God cares, and God will take care of justice. We don't have to retaliate or get even because our Lord is the captain of heaven's armies; He can definitely take care of it on His own! That frees us to live out the words of Romans 12:19-21:

> Dear friends, never take revenge. Leave that to the righteous anger of God. For the Scriptures say,
>
> > "I will take revenge;
> > I will pay them back,"
> > says the LORD.
>
> Instead,
>
> > "If your enemies are hungry, feed them.
> > If they are thirsty, give them something to drink.
> > In doing this, you will heap
> > burning coals of shame on their heads."
>
> Don't let evil conquer you, but conquer evil by doing good.

Gracious Words

We've talked a lot about the power of others' words and God's words, but before we wrap up, I want to talk about one more person's words: yours. Jesus said, "The standard you use in judging is the standard by which you will be judged" (Matthew 7:2). Before we go slamming others for evil words, you and I have a responsibility to make sure our own words are building others up. Writing this chapter has been convicting the snot out of me because I've been getting mighty lazy in my vocabulary and tone of voice lately. I've been careless with the words I've spoken to my friends and (especially) family. I haven't been cruel or anything, but things I've said have been low on the encouragement meter and high on the "I'm the center of my universe" end. Just being real. I need this reminder (maybe you do too?):

> A gracious woman gains respect,
> > but ruthless men gain only wealth.
> Your kindness will reward you,
> > but your cruelty will destroy you.
>
> PROVERBS 11:16-17

A *gracious* woman gains honor. The Hebrew word for "gracious" in verse 16, *khane*, describes "whatever is pleasant and agreeable."[2] Put simply, a girl who is nice to be around gains others' respect! So let's strive to be the kind of girl who uses her words to create a pleasant atmosphere, build others up, speak truth, and point out the beauty in those around her. Oh, and when we look at ourselves in the mirror? Let's allow kindness to win there, too, because cruelty—even to ourselves—will only destroy us.

We can be gracious about others' faults because we know we have our own. We can be gracious about our *own* faults because we trust what God says about us. We can stand tall and appreciate all the beauty God has created in us because others' words don't define us. Amen?

> Jesus, the way You love me leaves me breathless! Your words about me make me want to become all that You see in me. You are beautiful, and I'm so thankful You've chosen to chase after my love. It's Yours for the taking. I value You above everything, and I trust Your words more than anyone else's. Even though it's hard some days, I choose to believe that I am as beautiful as You say I am. I can't wait to spend ever after with You! Amen.

Discussion Questions

1. *Can you think of any insecurities you battle today that started from someone else's words? Write about them in your journal, and ask God to help you get the right perspective about those insecurities.*

2. Is the voice in your head encouraging or a mean word ninja?

3. What choices do you have when someone speaks cruel words to you?

4. Finish this sentence: How much you value someone dictates how much you will value their _____.

5. What has God said about you?

6. Do you believe God's words? Do you live as though you believe them?

7. *Would you say you are known for using your words to build others up, tear them down, or somewhere in between?*

8. *What rewards do we get when we use gracious and kind words?*

Refuse to Take a Compliment

DIRECTIONS: When someone does say you're beautiful, shoot that compliment down like a fighter jet. They're obviously crazy (or you don't want to be snooty), so let them know why they're dead wrong by blocking, dodging, or downplaying any and all compliments.

As we've already seen, people can say some pretty mean things. But thankfully, not everything others say about us is negative. If we listen carefully, we might hear a compliment (or two, or many) from the people around us. And those compliments just might help convince us of the beauty right under our noses.

You'd think that we girls—girls who *want* others to think we're beautiful—would be thrilled to hear a compliment, especially from a member of the opposite sex! We *are* thrilled, aren't we? But in one of the great upside-down mysteries of life, girls have a *really* hard time accepting compliments. In fact, we are notorious compliment killers.

An Australian journalist wrote a piece about this great mystery that had me rolling with laughter (and blushing— you know, the way you do when you totally get called out on something). He said,

> It's easy for a woman to compliment a man. All men secretly believe themselves to be gorgeous, and so will accept any compliment without question. Describe a bloke as "handsome beyond belief, a stud-muffin with a brilliant mind, possibly the best-looking bloke ever born," and he'll merely wonder why you weren't more effusive.
>
> By contrast, all women secretly believe they are ugly and will test any compliment, rather like a lawyer for the defence when confronted with a piece of dubious evidence.
>
> "Really? You think that? Why do you put it that way? Are you sure you don't need glasses?" . . .
>
> Compliment your female friend on her appearance and inevitably a strange look passes over her face. It is a look that means you are either blind or insane. She's not sure which. But you just said she was attractive, which proves you are some form of peculiar.[1]

It's so true it's funny! We're just not sure what to do when someone notices our beauty and tells us so. It's too bad, really. We're missing out on some well-meaning, life-giving compliments because of our awkwardness about them. One teen guy I know commented,

Girls are too defensive these days when it comes to looks and will either refuse to take a compliment or will take [it] as an advance on them. Sometimes I wish that I could just tell a girl how beautiful she is, but I rarely find the courage to tell her because I know she'll just shoot me down.[2]

I wonder how many guys feel that way. Man, is this refusing compliments stuff backfiring on us! What girl wouldn't want to hear a guy tell her he thinks she's beautiful "just because," without any ulterior motives? But because we haven't learned to accept compliments gracefully, we've convinced guys that we don't want to hear them. Even when they are genuine and innocent. Even when they are *true*.

Compliment Killers

We, my friend, are trained compliment killers. With sniper-like skill, we assassinate compliments from guys, girls, parents, teachers, grocery clerks, Internet friends, and random people on the street. And we usually squash a compliment one of three ways.

We block it.

Like a soccer goalie or middle blocker in volleyball, sometimes we completely block a compliment. We see it coming, and we block as if we're playing the final game of the season and we're down 2-to-1. If someone tells us we look nice, we fire back with some variation of "You're wrong." Here's how a conversation might sound:

> **Friend 1:** "Your hair looks nice today."
> **Friend 2:** "Ugh! No way—it looks terrible! I just rolled out of bed this morning. It's a total mess."
> **Friend 1** (feeling obligated to give another compliment to convince Friend 2 she meant the first one): "Oh. Well, I like the messy chic look you've got going on."
> **Friend 2:** (Laughs awkwardly)

We dodge it.

When we dodge a compliment, we pretend it didn't happen and change the subject as soon as possible. It's like trying to avoid getting pelted in a game of dodgeball (except this is totally irrational because no one is trying to hurt or disqualify you—they're actually trying to be nice!).

> **Friend 1:** "You're a good soccer player."
> **Friend 2** (ignoring Friend 1 said anything and quickly changing the subject): "Uh, are you coming to the game tonight?"
> **Friend 1** (feeling awkward for apparently making Friend 2 feel awkward): "No, I don't think I can make it."
> **Friend 2:** "Oh, that's too bad." (Followed by an awkward silence)

We downplay it.

Downplaying a compliment comes the most naturally to me. How is it done? Well, instead of telling the person they are plain wrong (blocking the compliment), I throw out facts that minimize my role in whatever the person is admiring. In other words, if they like it, I probably didn't have much to do with it. Here's an example:

> **Friend 1:** "That dress looks great on you."
> **Friend 2:** "Yeah, I got it for like fifty cents at a thrift store."
> **Friend 1** (now feeling obligated to compliment Friend 2 on her bargain-hunting skills): "No way! That's really cool. You must be an awesome thrift shopper then."
> **Friend 2:** "I just have to get really good deals because I'm broke all the time." (Followed by an awkward moment of silence)

When we block, dodge, or downplay a compliment, we end up just dropping awkward bombs on what would have been a really nice moment. So instead of trying so hard to be humble, maybe we should just *be* humble, by thinking of others instead of ourselves! In the world of compliments, that means thinking of the other person instead of how embarrassed we are.

Why Can't We Accept a Compliment?

So why do we have such a hard time accepting compliments? I've been chewing on that lately, and I think it comes down to one of two reasons: either we honestly don't think we deserve the compliment or we *do* believe the compliment but don't want to appear all high on ourselves by acknowledging that we actually believe it. Am I on to something?

On the one hand, some of us have a hard time seeing anything good in ourselves, so we assume no one else can either. We're still learning to trust what God says about us. Do you remember what He says? If not, this should refresh your memory. God says:

> You are My treasured possession.
> Deuteronomy 7:6

> I made your body beautiful and complex, and I did a masterful job!
> Psalm 139:14

> In My eyes, you are without fault. You are perfect!
> Ephesians 1:4

> Even before I made the world, I loved you and chose you to be Mine.
> 1 Thessalonians 1:4; Ephesians 1:4

You are a child of the light—My light.
Ephesians 5:8

You are a citizen of heaven; you belong with Me.
Philippians 3:20

I have bought you back from death and forgiven you for everything you've ever done.
Ephesians 1:7

You are a beautiful, new creation!
2 Corinthians 5:17

When someone gives you a compliment, he or she is just acknowledging that God did a fantastic job in creating you! So don't shirk it. Embrace the words as sweet echoes of your Maker's voice—as His telling you what you're still learning to believe yourself.

On the flip side, others of us worry that if we accept a compliment, we're being conceited. We don't want to "wear pride like a jeweled necklace" (Psalm 73:6) because we know that it's the worst accessory. But we've got one thing wrong: accepting a compliment doesn't mean we're prideful! It's absolutely possible to acknowledge God's handiwork without being conceited. Remember what we learned back in step #3: it's not prideful to agree that God did a good job on something, even when that "something" is you! Being confident in His handiwork is one way we can shoot glory His way.

How to Accept a Compliment

So, how *should* we accept a compliment?

Is there a way to respond to a compliment that will show we are (1) confident in who God says we are and (2) humble? Yes! And I literally *just* saw it in action.

Today I happen to be writing at my all-time favorite, best hole-in-the-wall-coffee-shop-slash-eatery of all time, The French Press. (The portabella pita and raspberry oatmeal pancakes are both to die for! If you visit me, I promise to take you.) As I was sipping down the last of my giant mug of "thin mint" tea, I witnessed the coolest little exchange. At the table next to me, a mom and daughter were enjoying some of those raspberry pancakes I mentioned, lost in conversation. As they were talking, a young man walked over and said to the daughter, "I'm sorry to interrupt you while you're eating, but I just wanted to tell you that I think you're incredibly beautiful."

I held my breath. How would she respond? He was definitely right. The girl he was admiring *was* beautiful, with caramel-brown skin, big brown eyes, and a head of curly, honey-highlighted hair. But would she see it? Would she tell him he was crazy or ask if he needed glasses? I was overcome with relief when I heard her words:

"Thank you."

Her simple response was exactly right.

They exchanged names and a handshake, and then her admirer left the table with a simple, "Have a nice day."

I can pretty much guarantee she's not going to have a nice day. She is going to have a walkin'-on-air kind of day—a shoulders-held-back and singing-at-the-sky kind of day. After the drive-by compliment, she didn't stop smiling for a full five minutes. She gushed, "How sweet" and "I'm blushing!" to her mom, who I imagine was just as happy for her daughter as I was.

Oh, the power of a simple compliment when it's received with humble thankfulness!

Because she just said thank you (instead of blocking, dodging, or downplaying his words), she not only prevented an incredibly awkward moment but also gave that gutsy guy the confidence to go on and compliment another beautiful gal when the opportunity arises. We can all be thankful for that! Who knows—maybe it will be *you*.

When someone gives you a compliment, believe it, embrace it, give God the glory, and then say thank you. Trust me, those two little words will go a long way.

Do you remember the verses we saw at the end of the previous chapter? They totally apply here too:

A gracious woman gains respect,
  but ruthless men gain only wealth.
Your kindness will reward you,
  but your cruelty will destroy you.

PROVERBS 11:16-17

When someone gives you a compliment, a simple thank-you is a gracious and kind response. And your kindness (in not blocking, dodging, or downplaying) will reward you: You'll feel like the beautiful girl that you are!

Jesus said that "it is more blessed to give than to receive" (Acts 20:35), so let's not rob our friends, family, and acquaintances of the joy they get from *giving* compliments by refusing to *accept* them. Deal? And while we're at it, let's tap into that joy ourselves by freely spoiling others with kind compliments of our own. Why don't you and I commit to being gracious and kind to others by upping our compliment ante? Let's look for ways to tell others just how beautiful they are, with no hard feelings, jealousy, or expectations. Just because, and with no strings attached. And then let's savor the joy that follows!

Jesus, You gave me the greatest compliment of all time when You said I was worth dying for. Because of who You say I am, God, I know I can accept others' compliments too. Teach me how to do it graciously, staying humble in my heart as I give You the glory. And show me ways I can bless the people around me with life-giving compliments too. I want to be Your salt and light in this world, God. Amen.

Discussion Questions

1. *Take a minute to think about the last time someone gave you a strings-free compliment. How did you respond?*

2. *Why do we have a hard time accepting compliments?*

3. *What are three "techniques" we use to avoid accepting them? Can you think of any others?*

4. *Which technique do you use most often?*

5. *What's one simple, humble way to accept a compliment?*

6. *How does it bless others when we thankfully accept their kind words about us (hint: see Acts 20:35)?*

7. *Who is one person you can compliment today?*

View Your Body as a Power Tool

One day as I walked through my local bookstore, the title on the cover of *Seventeen* magazine caught my eye.[1] The glowing pink letters read like a neon sign across Selena Gomez's bare midsection: "GIRL POWER!" The brown beauty held her bright pink leather jacket wide open to reveal a midriff top with the word "CONFIDENT" stretched across her chest. Her easygoing, wide smile and windblown locks were the picture of coolness, as always. A sidebar read, "#1 Selena! How She Makes Her Own Rules In Life—And Love!"

The cover caught my eye because I'd been chewing on the subtle ways that advertising affects us. *Seventeen* was banking on the fact that every teen girl who saw that cover was going to connect to the message and want to buy their magazine. The cover story was "The 17 Most Powerful Girls 21 & Under." It's incredibly smart marketing, and *Seventeen* isn't the only one to capitalize on girls' desire for power.

I've got to stop here and clarify one thing: I'm all about girls' rights and encouraging my fellow females to go for their dreams. I know what a privilege it is to live in a country where girls are treated as equals and given the same rights and opportunities as men. In some parts of the world, girls are looked down on—even aborted—just for being girls. I myself am a confident, hardworking gal who has been able to do a lot of things and go a lot of places because I'm no doormat (but mostly because of God's grace in my life). However, I think we're in danger of missing out on God's best when we translate that go-getter attitude into the world of romance and marriage—when we have a my-way-right-away attitude toward guys. Unfortunately, when I look at pop culture, *that's* the kind of power that's being marketed. Here are a couple more examples so you can see what I mean.

In one Armani ad, a good-looking lad sleeps on his back in the middle of a jungle (on top of a banana leaf, of course, so he doesn't spoil his designer khakis). A woman (who looks as though she hasn't eaten in months) stands over him with one foot strategically placed so that the heel of her gold stiletto is right above the most vulnerable part of the man's body (if you know what I mean). She's got both hands on her bikini-clad hips, and it appears as if she's either about to eat the camera or is in some serious pain (hard to tell which). She looks like a female Columbus, conquering the New World.

In a G-Unit ad, three hot divas are strolling down the street. They've got the hip sway and the tight/short/low clothes that practically shout, "Don't mess with us. We're unstoppable!" While they walk, each one of them eats a Popsicle. Strange but no big deal—until you look closer. Take a closer look, and their frozen treat turns out to be an ice cream shaped like a guy's face, with his green hat tipped to one side. These sexy girls are eating guy pops!

Seventeen advertises that you should make your own rules in love (ignoring God and His rules about love, which are for our good!). Armani says that if you wear his clothes, you'll be able to conquer any guy you want. If you wear G-Unit, you, too, can make your crush as helpless as a melting popsicle in your hand. Are you catching the trend?

Here's the thing: Not only are these companies telling you that you can and should have power over guys but they're showing that the way to do it is to bare more of your body. In every single "power ad" I've come across, the girls are dressed to reveal as much skin and sultry curves as possible. The message is clear: Dressing sexy will give you power over guys. And guess what? They're right—at least in part. I'll explain . . .

Intoxicating

Ask any guy, and he'll tell you that a woman's body is the most beautiful thing on the planet. (I didn't believe it until

I actually asked. Yep, it's true!) That shouldn't surprise us. We already know that God made Eve to be Adam's beautiful counterpart. Do you remember those unique characteristics about your body that make you distinctly woman? (If not, give a quick glance at page 5.) You are beautiful just by being a girl. Well, He also gave guys a special capacity to be completely drawn to, enraptured by, and undone because of a woman's bare curves. We see it in the Bible (think David and Bathsheba or Sampson and Delilah), and it's just as true today.

If I walked around my house in a tight, low-cut dress, my darling husband would be putty, smitten, able to think about nothing else than seeing the rest of my body. It's crazy, right?

A woman's body holds incredible power over a man.

A woman's love is intoxicating and captivating (see pretty much all of Song of Solomon and Proverbs 5:18-20 for further proof). We have God to thank for that! But like so many of God's good designs and gifts, even our captivating nature has been muddied by sin, which leads me back to those ads and to another question: How do advertisers know that they can get us to buy their product by promising us power?

The sad truth is that we *do* want to have power over guys. We know that our bodies have a powerful effect on men, and we're tempted to use that sway to control how they see us, treat us, and feel about us. It's not just our generation, in case you're wondering. Women have had that same desire for a long, long time—in fact, since the beginning of time.

When Adam and Eve sinned, God was forced to punish

them. Do you remember what consequence, or "curse," God gave Eve? Pain in childbirth. (Oh boy, do you have a lot to look forward to!) But there was a second part to the curse:

Then he said to the woman,

> "I will sharpen the pain of your pregnancy,
>   and in pain you will give birth.
> *And you will desire to control your husband,*
>   but he will rule over you."

GENESIS 3:16, EMPHASIS ADDED

Part of sin's curse is a desire to control men—to have power over them. Advertisers know they can get us to buy their products by promising us power because, deep down, we want it!

When God designed Adam, Eve, and marriage, he gave them equal worth but different roles. He gave men the role of leading, protecting, and providing. He gave the woman the role of childbearing, nurturing, and helping Adam. (These are general roles. I'm not saying that girls aren't good leaders or guys can't nurture. I don't have the space to go into depth here, but if you'd like to dig deeper on this subject, I can point you in a good direction at www.LifeLoveandGod.com.) The power struggle doesn't start once we get married. Oh, no—it starts way before that! Because of our sin nature, our desire for power over guys starts as soon as we're old enough to notice they're cute and want a relationship with one of them. I was in elementary school when the thirst for power started. How

I would have loved to walk over to my first crush, snap my fingers, and say, "Like me!" and then—bing!—have him follow me around like a puppy the rest of second grade.

This is why we have such a hard time waiting for guys to pursue *us*. We know what we want, and we want it when we want it. We want to be in control of the person, the pace, and the promise of a relationship. Even though we long for guys to take such delight in us that they'd be willing to do whatever it took to pursue our hearts, we get impatient when we're not getting what we want when we want it. So we start manipulating situations to be around them, to get them to notice us. We try to take the reins to move things along. That's the way I operated, anyway, for much of my dating years, and I know I'm not alone. Just ask Armani.

Wouldn't we all like that kind of power? That's why we love songs and shows and magazine articles and advertisements that portray women as being in charge of their lives and their love.

But God didn't design girls to have power over guys; He designed us to live in harmony with one another. First Corinthians 11:11-12 says,

> Among the Lord's people, women are not independent of men, and men are not independent of women. For although the first woman came from man, every other man was born from a woman, and everything comes from God.

Woman came from man, but man comes from woman. God designed us to live and love in harmony with each other. And when we do things His way—when we embrace the heart of a servant, no matter our gender, relationships work really well. Satan doesn't want that! Satan knows that when things work the way God designed them to work, that's bad business for him. So he does everything he can to turn God's designs upside down—to destroy harmony, to break up families, to convince us that our bodies and sex are just power tools we can use to get what we want. Satan wants to undermine our dignity and lead us down a path of sexual sin.

What advertisers don't tell you—and what Satan certainly doesn't want you to know—is that another danger in using your body to exercise power over guys is that you'll be seen as just a body. A girl who flaunts her goods will most definitely get more attention and even relationships with guys. She'll get what she wants. Sort of. I say sort of because they won't be the kind of relationships *she's really after*. We want to be desired. We want guys to be attracted to our bodies. But even deeper than that, we want to be desired for our souls. We want guys to see our hearts and prize them and protect them and cherish them! When we market our bodies on the cheap (with our clothes, words, and actions), we are likely to attract guys who are looking for only a body and the right to have unrestricted *access* to that body, not a commitment.

So let's talk about clothes for a minute. I think we girls get a bad rap sometimes. People often assume that if we're showing skin, it's because we want to be sexual. But I think it actually goes back to our quest to feel beautiful.

Copying "Cute"

I have a hunch that one of the main reasons we dress the way we do is because we define our "cute factor" by how closely we match something we've seen in print or on a screen. If my clothes, hair, and makeup match a picture I saw on online or in a magazine, I feel beautiful. And because most of the looks out there revolve around making guys look twice, we dress the part without thinking twice.

In our defense, because we don't always get turned on by seeing a guy in shorts, it doesn't cross our minds that a guy might get turned on by seeing *our* legs in shorts. But guys are more visual when it comes to that stuff, and even though we might not completely understand, as God's daughters we have a responsibility to try to get where they're coming from.

Now, if you're afraid I'm going to bust out a ruler and start giving regulations about inseam lengths, you can exhale. My job isn't to give you hard-and-fast rules about what's modest and what isn't. There are so many factors that go into modesty: our culture, the weather, our parents' rules, where we're going in those clothes, and so on. My goal is simply to challenge you to question why you choose the clothes you do and ask yourself whether you're putting yourself or others first in your clothing choices. As girls who love God, we have a responsibility to consider others and look out for their good (see Philippians 2:3-4). One huge way we can care for the guys in our lives is by limiting our "freedom" for their sakes. Galatians 5:13 says,

> You have been called to live in freedom, my brothers and sisters. But don't use your freedom to satisfy your sinful nature. Instead, use your freedom to serve one another in love.

When I read that verse, this is what I hear: "Hey, Jessie, you might be free to dress how you want to, but don't put looking 'cute' over caring about others. Instead, use your wardrobe freedom to serve the guys around you by keeping temptation to a minimum." I'll have a side of conviction with that, thank you very much! I wish I could say I had this all under wraps, but I still wrestle from time to time with where my responsibility stops and a guy's starts. One thing I'm 100 percent sure of though: When I sacrifice my rights for others in the name of love (in any area of life), that's when my heart finds the most peace. So when it comes to clothes, I ask God to check my heart's motives and give Him veto power in my closet. Are you up for the challenge?

Modest doesn't have to mean drab! If you need some classy clothing inspiration, visit www.LifeLoveandGod.com/cool-stuff.

Attention!

I think there's another reason we're drawn to dress in less, and it also goes back to that desire to feel beautiful: We crave the attention we get when we dress that way because it makes us feel attractive.

Recap:
- A girl's body is beautiful.
- Guys are drawn to that beauty.

Because of those truths, girls who bare more skin or talk and act suggestively *do* get more attention. When a guy is drawn to a girl's body, he naturally wants to get close to it. He is attracted to her, flirts with her, and pays her attention. I'm sure you've seen this in action. Maybe you've experienced it yourself. I'll be the first to tell you that it feels mighty good to be on the receiving end of that attention. We feel liked, admired, and even desired.

The attention we get when we dress immodestly isn't healthy attention, mind you, but when we have deep, empty holes in our hearts that crave love and acceptance, we don't always see that truth. We convince ourselves that the extra attention is due to our kindness, charm, and witty comebacks, not the silhouette of our curves under our supertight shirt.

One girl blew me away with her brave honesty on this topic. I had been speaking to a group of teen girls about some of this stuff and she came up afterward to talk. She had obviously been listening and thinking very deeply about why she chose to dress the way she did. She said, "Do you know what I realized? I realized I'm an attention whore," and then quickly added, "Excuse my French." I don't think that's French, but who was I to argue? She bravely continued, "I crave that attention, and I don't know why." I was beyond proud of her for putting into words what so many of us girls struggle with. Even though we know we'd rather have more positive attention—such as for our brains, guts, or kindness—we still settle for less noble attention because we are broken people who want to be the center of attention.

First Corinthians 3:3 says,

> As long as you grab for what makes you feel good
> or makes you look important, are you really much
> different than a babe at the breast, content only
> when everything's going your way? (MSG)

If you've spent much time around babies, you can appreciate Paul's analogy here. Babies are adorable—so cute and smiley and chubby and sweet . . . until they're hungry. When a baby wants to eat, you're going to hear about it, and you're going to *keep* hearing about it until she gets what she wants! If we crave others' attention so bad that we're willing to do whatever it takes to get it—even treat our bodies like a power tool—according to the apostle Paul, we're really no different than a baby, content only when she gets what she wants.

In other words, if we're only content when all eyes are on us, then we've got a maturity problem. Ouch! As convicting as that is, Paul's right, isn't he? When you or I choose to dress to get attention, it reveals immaturity. It shows that we still have some growing up to do in the Lord.

Just in case you feel as though I'm pointing a finger, let me tell you, I was *totally* guilty of this. I'm a little embarrassed to admit some of the things I wore (and even got in trouble for wearing) as a teenager. And as long as we're keeping it real, this verse *still* convicts the junk out of me! I still crave attention. Left to my sinful nature, I want to be on center stage of my world, with all my family and friends looking up at me in adoration. It's ugly and it's wrong. In order for me to be content hanging out in the background, serving and loving others without recognition, I have to die to myself daily. So I'm right there with you when I ask, *Can we look at our own lives and say, "I'm content, even when all eyes aren't on me"?* That's what I want to be able to say. How about you?

Just a Body?

If we view our bodies as power tools—as things we can use to get guys to do what we want—we cheapen the value and worth God has given us as human beings created in His image. A tool is a thing. An *object*. It's something to use until it doesn't have use and then take to the junkyard. And if you view your body that way, there's no way you can embrace the true beauty and value it has. Does that make sense? A girl who views her body as a power tool over guys is going to keep on leveraging her body to get what she wants, even if it leads her into sin. And a girl who views her body as a tool won't object when a guy treats her like an object because she already views herself as one.

So if you want to feel ugly—if you want to have a cheap view of yourself—then dress and act sexually to grab guys' attention. Use what you've got to get what you want, and don't question what kind of attention you're really getting. But if you want to see yourself as the beautiful treasure you are—a precious daughter of the King—then act and dress the part. Let your attitude shine with grace and humility. And let the clothes you wear show the world that the most beautiful parts of you—of your body *and* of your heart—are reserved for your future husband alone. You may not get as much attention or as many boyfriends as girls who dress in less, but you'll have two things even better: God's approval and your dignity.

> God, You know how tempting it can be for us girls to leverage our beauty to gain power over guys or to get our way in relationships. Help me battle that desire and walk humbly with You instead. I want to be a girl with dignity and show respect for myself in the way I dress, act, and talk around others. Nudge my heart when I'm out of line. Deal? I love You, Lord. Amen.

Discussion Questions

1. Why do advertisers try to sell their products by promising us power over guys?

2. Why do we want to have power over members of the opposite sex?

3. How can using our bodies like power tools backfire on us? (How can it actually make us feel ugly?)

4. Do you see any ways that you try to control or have power over guys? If so, write about them in your journal. Then ask God to show you a better way.

5. How do we usually decide what outfits are cute or in? What would be a good standard to use?

6. *Do you ever dress to catch guys' attention? If so, why do you think you do that?*

7. *According to 1 Corinthians 3:3, what does craving others' attention reveal about our hearts?*

STEP #7

Eat Junk and Diet, Diet, Diet

DIRECTIONS: Don't give a thought to what you eat. Fast food, candy, and soda should be your major food groups, and cut way back on "living foods," such as fruits and vegetables. If you become overweight, try the latest fad diet or cleanse. Repeat.

It was the first day the sun had come out—*really* come out—in an entire month. (That's only a slight exaggeration.) After a long winter, a sun sighting was a time to rejoice, especially for this Southern California native. I was borderline euphoric as I enjoyed the glorious rays, driving to a women's retreat where I was speaking that afternoon. The endorphins created by the sudden spring weather might be partially responsible for my decision to pay an exorbitant amount to have my truck washed at a fund-raiser. (Okay, maybe I was just too embarrassed to show up at the retreat in my mud-covered truck.) As I sat in the Albertsons parking lot, making small talk with the scrubbers, I watched a kid's mom unload lunch from her minivan. She made her way to the group with several large bags displaying the golden arches and placed them next to a stash of soft drinks. The teen girl I had been talking with—a cute blonde in pajama pants and a tank top—grabbed a double cheeseburger and a Rockstar energy drink from the bounty. In a hurry to get back to work, she scarfed down the burger in thirty-four seconds flat, chased it with the Rockstar, fixed her hair (using a car window as a mirror), and got back to scrubbing.

I know this isn't uncommon lunch fare for teens; in fact, I was one of the worst offenders. My freshman year of high school, my usual noon meal consisted of either a Frito boat or a pack of crumb-covered Hostess Donettes and a Sprite. (If my mother only knew!) By senior year, I had upgraded to a Twix candy bar and a blue Powerade. It seemed so harmless to me then; maybe it still does to you. But we in America (and people all over the world, really) are starting to see the consequences of all our on-the-go, ready-made junk-food indulgences.

Fast-Food Nation

It might seem kind of weird to be talking about healthy eating in a Christian book, but I'm convinced that God cares a lot about how well we take care of the bodies He has given us. (We'll talk more about that a little later.)

As a nation, our eating habits are out of control. It's not

just us, either; the whole world is falling off the health train. Check out the following stats:

69.2 %	Of U.S. adults are overweight or obese.[1]
> 33.3 %	Of U.S. teens are overweight or obese.[2]
> 2,800,000	People die each year, worldwide, because of bad eating habits and/or not enough exercise.[3]

How has it gotten so bad? A lot of complex reasons to be sure, including economics, sedentary lifestyles, and government subsidies on poor-quality food. But ultimately, the buck stops with us, doesn't it? The leading cause of these deaths is, after all, *eating*. More specifically, eating poorly. The culprits include eating "foods" like the Carl's Jr. breakfast burger: a goopy, greasy burger piled high with all sorts of artery-clogging items. Carl's advertises, "It's a coffee shop breakfast plate on a bun: one fried egg, hash browns, two slices of bacon, toasted bun, and beef patty." I feel they should have mentioned the ketchup shown dripping out of every nook and cranny, enough to be a food item all on its own, but maybe that part costs extra. I honestly don't know how that mess of a meal could stay on the bun, but apparently it's a big hit.

When I look at how the majority of us Americans (and much of the world) eat, I'm surprised we're not all Violet already. (No offense if your name *is* Violet. I'm referring to *Willy Wonka and the Chocolate Factory*, where the little girl with the chewing gum fancy blows up into a giant blueberry. The Oompa Loompas roll her around the room while singing a weird little song. Quite the visual. But I digress.) I'm convinced that God has a better plan for His daughters than for us to die of heart attacks, diabetes, or any of the other dozen deadly diseases caused by poor eating habits and lack of exercise.

Now, this is a book about beauty and, more specifically, how to feel beautiful. I'm a firm believer that a girl is beautiful whether she is carrying around extra pounds or not. *Truly.* Your beauty is not dependent on a number on a scale or fitting a certain size! God has beautifully designed us, but when we treat our bodies like human garbage disposals, we have a hard time seeing that beauty; we have a harder time believing Him.

Let me ask you a tough question: Do you think that some of your body-related insecurities stem from not taking care of the body God has given you by eating right? I know mine did. And from where I sit now, I can see a direct connection between those insecurities and the food I ate.

A Look in the Mirror

It's always hard to look in the mirror and own up to the truth, but as Socrates said, "The unexamined life is not worth living." So, before we go any further, I want you to take a little quiz to get a handle on your personal tendencies toward treats and eats. Circle whichever answers best describe your eating habits.

1. *If I joined you for lunch tomorrow, you'd offer to share your*
   A. Slice of pizza and a diet Coke
   B. Peanut butter and jelly sandwich and milk
   C. Spinach salad and water
   D. Snickers and Red Bull

2. *Which of the following most closely resembles your idea of a healthy meal?*
   A. A Chicken Selects Extra Value Meal from Mickey D's
   B. A home-cooked meal of spaghetti and garlic bread
   C. Grilled fish and wild rice
   D. Domino's Pizza

3. *When you go to the fridge or pantry for a snack, you're most likely to emerge with*
   A. A pudding cup or bag of chips
   B. A cereal bar or bowl of Lucky Charms
   C. An apple or other piece of fruit
   D. A scoop of Ben and Jerry's Chocolate Peanut Butter Fudge

4. *How many eight-ounce glasses of water do you drink a day? (Sodas don't count!)*
   A. 1 to 2
   B. 3 to 4
   C. 5 or more
   D. I don't drink water—it makes me thirsty.

5. *If someone asked you why you eat the way you do, you'd probably respond with*

   A. "I just eat whatever is easiest. I'm too busy to care."
   B. "I try to eat healthy food, but usually the chocolate screams louder."
   C. "I just feel better about myself when I eat right."
   D. "I tried eating healthy food once, but I broke out in a rash."

Okay, you know the drill. For every A answer, give yourself 1 point. Bs score 2 points, Cs get 3, and Ds get 0. I don't think I really have to write out the little score sheet. You've probably already guessed that unless you scored 14 or 15, you've got room to improve your food choices. (Don't we all?) Before this chapter is over, I'll give you some practical tips for eating better. In the meantime, let's talk about food in general: where it came from and why we eat it (two questions that could be answered in three words: "God" and "We're hungry." But I wouldn't be much of a writer if it didn't take me lots of words to answer simple questions!).

The Garden of Eatin'

Yes, we've spent an awful lot of time in the Garden of Eden already. However, we've got one more stop to make, because not only did Adam and Eve get created and fall in love in that beautiful oasis, they were also introduced to another of life's loves: food.

Then God said, "Look! I have given you every seed-bearing plant throughout the earth and all the fruit trees for your food."

GENESIS 1:29

And in that simple statement, God presented Adam and Eve with a banquet of good eats—a smorgasbord of tastes, textures, and tantalizing colors. I'm sure they figured out pretty quickly that their grumbling tummies meant they needed some nourishment. I wonder what they ate first. Oranges? Figs? Maybe some fresh veggies? I don't know. But I do know that it must have tasted heavenly. (Can you imagine tasting for the very first time?) And I also know that it didn't contain any preservatives, pesticides, refined sugar, or processed greases.

God is all-powerful, right? And He's super-creative, right? And when He designed the world He could have made it any way He wanted, right? Well, if all that's true, there must be a very good reason God didn't make a cheeseburger tree or rivers that flow Dr Pepper.

God said that the way He makes food—fresh, natural, and wholesome—is "very good" (see Genesis 1:11-12). Not only does He give us food with all sorts of nutrients that our bodies need for optimum health but He also put taste buds in our mouths so we can enjoy all the tasty treats He created. Amazing, don't you think?

RANDOM FOOD FACT

Did you know that Adam and Eve were the first vegetarians? That's right. Before they sinned (by eating the forbidden *fruit*, ironically), there was no death. No death meant no steaks, jerky, or ham sandwiches. Only *after* they were kicked out of the Garden did they begin using animals for food.

Everything God created is good. Too often we humans come along, thinking we can improve on His design, and end up messing everything up. When you think about it, most of our problems today are self-inflicted: pollution, war, crime, many sicknesses, and the list goes on and on. The same is true of food. God makes plants and trees to give us fruits and veggies and grains and all sorts of good stuff; then we come along and process, preserve, and package it until all the nutrients are gone and we're left with second-rate food that has little to no nourishment (but lots of potential for addiction). If we're going to break that cycle, first we have to change our view of food.

Fuel Injection

There's one basic difference between the way God designed us to eat food and the way we like to eat it. God gave us food primarily for fuel; it's an extra bonus when it tastes really good. We tend to eat food primarily for pleasure, and it's an extra bonus if it actually nourishes our bodies.

To see if this is true for you, think about the foods you've eaten so far today. What did you have for breakfast, lunch, snacks, dinner, and dessert? As you think about each item, ask yourself if you ate it primarily for fuel or for pleasure (or somewhere in between). Are you surprised by how often you tend to pick your food based on how it tastes?

Either here or in your journal, make a list of your ten favorite things to eat.

1.   6.
2.   7.
3.   8.
4.   9.
5.   10.

Now go back and put a line through all the foods that taste amazing but aren't really good for you (foods you primarily eat for pleasure, such as ice cream or pizza). Circle all the foods that make your body healthy and strong. Now, just because you put a line through an item doesn't mean you can never eat it! God isn't some old fogy in the sky telling us we shouldn't eat anything that tastes good. But if we want to feel our most beautiful, we should focus on eating foods the way God made them, in their most natural state, and eat the treats we love in moderation.

If you're anything like me, you probably need a little more convincing before you sign up for Healthy Living 101. So here are three big reasons—one each for your spiritual, emotional, and physical sides—to ditch the Standard American Diet (S.A.D., ironically) and get healthy instead.

Eating well honors God.

In the Old Testament, God had the Israelites build a big tent called the Tabernacle, and that's where God lived. But once Jesus died for our sins, ushering in the New Covenant, God didn't want a house built with hands anymore. Now He lives *in us*. Try to get your mind around that for a second. If you have made God the master of your life, His Spirit lives inside you. *You* are God's temple 2.0! First Corinthians 3:16-17 says,

> You realize, don't you, that you are the temple of
> God, and God himself is present in you? No one
> will get by with vandalizing God's temple, you can
> be sure of that. God's temple is sacred—and you,
> remember, *are* the temple. (MSG)

Our bodies are God's temple. Does that mean that if we eat a Cinnabon, we're "cinn-ing"? (Ba-dum-cha.) Thankfully, no! This verse isn't meant to scare us; it's meant to help us understand that God cares how we treat our bodies. He doesn't look down His nose at us every time we eat dessert, and He doesn't hold a measuring tape to our bodies while we sleep, but we honor Him when we treat our bodies well.

Eating well builds character.

> All athletes are disciplined in their training. . . .
> I discipline my body like an athlete, training it to
> do what it should.
>
> I CORINTHIANS 9:25, 27

To be disciplined means that *you* control your body, not the other way around. If you play sports, you probably understand this principle already. When you're training, you can't listen to your tired muscles and heaving chest. You tell your body, "Hey, listen up—guess who's in charge here! You're not going to die, Miss Thang, so suck it up and keep going!" (Okay, that's what *I* say. You might be a little nicer about it.) God is passionate about our freedom; He doesn't want us to be a slave to anything, which includes our senses. He wants us to enjoy the sense of taste, for example, but He doesn't want us to be mastered by it. Sometimes we should say no to certain foods, not because they're sinful but so we can remind our body that we're in charge, not our cravings.

A by-product of being disciplined in the way we eat is contentment. If you're not sure how those two go together, let me explain. When we're constantly overloading our taste buds with sweets, salt, and other yummy treats, we keep craving more. But when we use discipline and limit what we eat to healthy choices, a strange thing happens: We find that we can be completely satisfied without the junk. The apostle Paul taught that contentment with just the basics is a good thing.

In 1 Timothy 6:8, he wrote, "If we have enough food and clothing, let us be content." The basics are all we need, but sometimes we have to get *down* to the basics to realize that.

Eating well allows your body to shine.

Your body is made to run off of clean fuel. When you feed your body the kinds of foods God designed it to run on, it will function at its best. Don't underestimate how cool this is! Ten years ago, I started trading in my Frito boats and pleasure-first choices for healthier foods, and I've been amazed at how my body has responded. I'm talking about more energy, clearer skin, stronger muscles and bones, less sickness, healthier hair and nails, and sharper thinking. Feed it well, and your body will thank you!

Ten Tips for Eating Right

Now that we know where food came from and why we should (and shouldn't) eat it, here are a few practical tips I've learned over the years to help me stick to my guns. To truly look and feel your best, eating right has to be a lifestyle, not a fad you try out for a season and then donate to the Salvation Army. Pace yourself. And if you fudge a little every so often, remember that it's not the end of the world. Tomorrow is a new day!

#1: Don't use food as an escape.

God didn't make food to fill emotional holes in our hearts or to keep us busy when we're bored. Eating sweets when we're upset, browsing the snack cupboard when there's nothing else to do, and social eating are all unhealthy food escapes. Breaking an emotional eating habit takes determination, and it takes turning to God with your pain instead of to the fridge.

> *If you're ready to break free from emotional eating, I highly recommend arming yourself with a great study such as* Made to Crave for Young Women.[4]

#2: Don't torture yourself.

I have the willpower of a starving elephant trapped in a field of peanuts. I'd like to *think* I'm strong and self-controlled and all that, but put me in a house with chocolate-chip cookies or salt-and-vinegar chips, and they'll be gone before dinner. I know this about myself, so I no longer keep them stocked in the cupboards. Know your limits; then replace the tempting foods with healthy ones. (You might need to solicit your parents' help on this one. If you tell them your reasons, I'm sure they'll be happy to help you on your road to healthy eating. They may even join you!)

#3: Eat just enough.

Live by the maxim "Don't eat until you're full; just eat until you aren't hungry anymore." Most of us are blessed not to have to wonder where we're going to find food tomorrow. We know that when we next get hungry, there will be food enough. So there's no point in stuffing yourself at any meal. These two verses are worth memorizing:

> A righteous man eats until he is satisfied.
> PROVERBS 13:25, HCSB

> Give me enough food to live on,
>   neither too much nor too little.
> If I'm too full, I might get independent,
>   saying, "God? Who needs him?"
> PROVERBS 30:8-9, MSG

#4: Keep a water bottle with you.

This one's pretty self-explanatory. If you've always got water on hand, you'll not only stay hydrated but also eat less and drink soda less frequently. I don't go anywhere without my dinged-up, stainless steel SIGG bottle, and I hardly ever have to buy a drink. Bonus points: When you *do* get stuck without liquid, choose water over juice, sports drinks, or soda.

#5: Just say no.

We already talked about this one under the emotional benefits of healthy eating, but it's so important I have to mention it again. Discipline yourself to say no to good treats every so often just to remind your body who's in charge and to practice the fine art of self-control.

#6: Say good-bye to cravings.

Your cravings work a bit like the custom settings on your phone. Once you set your phone's ringtone to "What Does the Fox Say?" (not that you would *do* that), your phone will keep singing out a shrill "Wa-pa-pa-pa-pa-pa-pow!" every time the phone rings until you change the settings. Your body is kind of like that. It remembers the last thing you ate, and it wants it—and wants it some more—until you reset your cravings.

Here's an example: Last night I was totally PMS-ing and splurged on a couple of oatmeal-raisin cookies I had made my hubby the other day. Guess what I was craving first thing this morning? Yep—those cookies were calling my name with reckless abandon while I made breakfast. If I eat salt, I'll crave chips; if I have those delicious breadsticks from Olive Garden, I won't be able to get them out of my mind. The best way to break a cycle of cravings is to reset your palate. How? The only way I've found is to just say no to whatever it is you're craving. Keep saying no, and before you know it, you won't even be thinking about those cookies!

#7: Plan ahead.

Remember the girl from the car wash? She ate what she did for lunch because she was rushed. Eating right takes planning; you have to think about what you're going to eat *before* you're starving and ready to scarf down anything in front of you. If you don't already, consider packing your own lunch and snacks so you don't have to decide what to eat while you're hungry and staring at a fast-food menu. The best time to pack your food is right after you've eaten breakfast or after dinner the night before, when you aren't hungry. It's amazing how much more wisely we choose when our stomach isn't grumbling.

#8: Stay true to God's food.

Eat foods as close to the way God made them as possible. I like to call it "original food." For example, instead of a packaged fruit cup, try an actual piece of fruit, such as an apple or peach. Instead of an energy bar, reach for a handful of almonds and raisins. If a food is alive, or was a short time ago, you have a winner. On the other hand, think twice if you can't pronounce most of the items on the ingredients list. Remember, God made food the way He did for a reason. He knows what our bodies need for optimum health and function and made foods to meet those needs. It's best to trust Him and not alter His food design too much.

#9: Find a friend.

You'll be more motivated and successful and have more fun in this process if you join forces with a friend. Studies show that accountability is a huge factor for success when it comes to just about every positive life change, including healthy eating.

#10: Ask God for help.

Not only should you find human help, you should solicit divine help too! This should be a no-brainer, but unfortunately we often forget that God actually *cares* about our health and well-being. Ask Him to help you stay disciplined and motivate you to eat right for the right reasons.

I could talk for hours about nutrition and food, and if we ever get a chance to meet in person, you might have to stop me from doing just that! Because my own life has been transformed by better nutrition, I'm passionate about girls understanding the connection between what they eat and how their bodies respond. As I've learned to eat foods the way God made them, enjoy treats as just that, and focus on foods more for fuel than pleasure, I have found freedom I didn't know was possible. And you, too, can live a life free from worry when it comes to food and your weight.

Next we'll talk about another very important part of keeping our bodies healthy for God's glory: exercise. (Don't worry, it won't be *too* painful!) But before we end this chapter, let me pray for us:

> God, thank You for making such amazing food for us to eat. You are so creative! Help me to be disciplined in the way I eat and to take care of my body to honor You in this temple. I want to be healthy inside and out so others can see who You are and what I can accomplish when You're in control of my life. Amen.

Discussion Questions

1. *On a scale of 1 to 5, how healthy are your eating habits (with 1 being "I take better care of my hamster" and 5 being "I'm in tip-top shape")?*

2. If you had designed the world of human food, what would you have done differently? Be creative!

3. What are your favorite tastes? Do you like things sweet or salty? Sour or rich? Which foods has God made ("original foods") that taste that way?

4. According to 1 Corinthians 3:16-17, why is it so important that we take good care of our bodies?

5. Which of the three reasons for healthy eating—spiritual, emotional, and physical—motivates you most? Why?

6. Pull out your journal and write down any of the "Ten Tips for Eating Right" that you can work on this week.

Adore or Ignore Exercise

DIRECTIONS: Take an extreme view of exercise. Make training for your sport or a perfectly toned body your greatest goal in life. Or, if you don't think you're the athletic type, view exercise as torture and avoid it at all costs. Either extreme will do nicely to make sure you feel your worst.

It was a Tuesday night at my local gym. The TVs aired their usual second-rate sitcoms, the hum of the machines sounded like a swarm of mosquitoes in July, and the place smelled like a sweaty rubber mat. Yep, pretty much a normal night at the gym. Oh, except that I was wearing trendy workout clothes for once (you know, the ones I regretted buying at the beginning of the book). At least I felt cute knowing that everyone was mistaking me for Kate Hudson while I sweat.

While I was suffering through sit-ups outside the Zumba class window, I stole a sideways glance at the girl working out next to me. She was a petite brunette with glasses, probably in her early twenties, wearing a tank top and spandex shorts.

She caught my eye because she didn't seem to be suffering *at all* through her workout. In fact, she was doing some killer ab moves with a medicine ball as though it were the easiest thing in the world. I couldn't help but wonder whether I would pull or break something if I tried to do the same moves.

Now, if I were in close proximity to that girl anywhere other than the gym—at church, the grocery store, at a bus stop, wherever—I would have introduced myself, got to chatting, and probably ended the convo with a hug. (Don't judge me—I'm a hugger, people.) *Any*where else, I would have been cheery and warm and welcoming. But at the gym, it's like it's against the rules to smile or make eye contact or appear anything other than serious and intimidating. Most of us are so focused on ourselves—making sure we look athletic and toned and *not* awkward—that we never really think to reach out to the people around us. We're simultaneously worried that someone might be looking at us and hoping that they *are* noticing us (and those toned triceps we've been working on). Am I right? At the gym, guys strut around like beefy roosters, and girls are busy making tally marks on their comparison scorecards. It's no surprise that the gym culture is one of the most common reasons people give for avoiding exercise. They equate exercise with hanging out at the gym, and who wants to willingly subject themselves to the picture I've just painted? If you're one of those people who would rather watch a Power Rangers marathon than go to the gym, I hope this next part of the story will encourage you to take a second look at exercise.

After my workout, I noticed the same girl—the brunette with the glasses—just a few lockers down from mine, and I thought, *This is dumb, Jessie. Get over yourself and just say hi already.* So I faced my fear of getting kicked out of the gym for breaking the "no friendliness" rule and introduced myself.

Her name was Valentina, and she happened to be the nicest person on the planet. Turns out she moved here from Russia when she was young, works with toddlers, and loves God. When she asked questions, I could tell she genuinely cared. She is one of those people you could spend two minutes with and feel as though you've known your whole life. In fact, we were so wrapped up in conversation that we didn't notice the towel-clad girls dripping wet and waiting to get to the lockers we were blocking with our impromptu friendship. Oops?

Anyway, somewhere in our conversation, I told her she looked like she knew what she was doing out there with that medicine ball and asked whether she had a background in sports. She said yes and told me the following story.

Just before her freshman year of high school, Valentina decided to try out for the volleyball team. The first day of summer tryouts, she showed up in her workout clothes and knee pads, ready to get to work. The only problem? She wasn't exactly sure where to go. She wandered around campus until she finally saw a group of kids stretching in a circle. Relieved, she plopped down with the group and started following along. A few minutes later, the coach announced that they were going to take a little warm-up run to the red church and back. She didn't see any red church, but not wanting to sound dumb, she just went with it. *Eight miles later*, she got back to the school. Turns out, Valentina had accidentally joined the cross-country team! She was too embarrassed to tell anyone, so she stuck with it the whole season. And the next. And the next! She ran four years of cross-country, by mistake. (And she never once played volleyball.)

Back at our lockers, I couldn't stop laughing. I was *crying* from laughter. Not only was it the funniest sports-related story I had ever heard, the way she told it was classic. And I never would have heard it if I hadn't stepped out of my comfort zone at the gym that night.

Gyms—and sports teams, tennis clubs, and the local basketball court—don't have to be intimidating if we start looking at the people around us as *people*. We hurt only ourselves when we let our insecurities keep us from enjoying the benefits of all the exercise options out there. And that's why I share my story about Valentina. I'm not necessarily trying to convince you to join a gym. But if you're one of the many girls who are intimidated by the thought of joining a sports team, enrolling in a rock-climbing class, or taking a board to the local skate park, I want to help you think through *why*. Is your dislike for exercise (if you have one) because you're afraid of what others might think about you or because you think going to a gym is the only way to get exercise? Maybe you just aren't sure where to start?

Whatever your objections, I hope the benefits of exercise will coax you to give it a shot (or another shot, if this ain't your first rodeo). We're going to talk about some of those benefits in a minute, but first I think we should spend a sec talking about balance.

The Exercise Extremists

It's really easy for people to fall into one of two extremes in how they view exercise. It seems to me that a lot of girls either make exercise their god or treat it like the plague. Both ends of the spectrum take something that's good in moderation—either exercise or rest—to the extreme, until it's no longer healthy.

On one side, we have the sports fanatics. This type of girl understands that her body is meant to move, and she wants her body to be in good physical condition. Those are both good things. But staying in shape can sometimes morph into an all-important god, and before she knows it, she is spending more time working out or playing sports than eating and sleeping combined (let alone spending time with the *true* God). She feels immense guilt for missing a workout or (heaven forbid) skipping a season of organized athletics. Ironically, her quest for health becomes unhealthy.

On the other side of the spectrum are the gymophobes. This type of girl doesn't even want to think about fitness. Exercise, in her humble opinion, is a fate worse than death. She wonders who in her right mind would inflict pain on herself and call it fun. The thought of exercising brings to mind images of trainer Jillian Michaels (of *The*

Biggest Loser fame) barking orders and bringing grown men to tears. Sometimes the gymophobe feels insecure about her weight, so she jokes about hating exercise or being too uncoordinated for athletics of any kind. Maybe she even looks down on the sports fanatics for being so extreme. Her lack of interest in physical activity has taken her to the other unhealthy extreme.

Obviously, exercise shouldn't become an idol in our lives. God makes it clear that we are to have no other gods besides Him—not the Buddha *or* exercise-bike kinds. That's the very first of the Ten Commandments He gave to Moses (see Exodus 20:3). At the same time, we've already seen that the Bible refers to our bodies as the temple of the Holy Spirit, so we should take care of them. Remember these verses?

> You realize, don't you, that you are the temple of
> God, and God himself is present in you? No one
> will get by with vandalizing God's temple, you can
> be sure of that. God's temple is sacred—and you,
> remember, *are* the temple.
> I CORINTHIANS 3:16-17, MSG

As God's set-apart living space, we honor Him when we take care of the bodies He has given us. In the previous chapter, we talked about how we can do that with the food we eat. Well, we can also honor Him through exercise if we find a healthy balance between the two exercise extremes.

Before we get to those benefits of exercise I promised, I want to connect the dots between the foods we eat and our need for exercise. Put simply, your body needs only so many calories a day. Anything extra, and your body will store the excess for a rainy day[1] (in those lovely little fat cells we all know and adore). When you eat primarily for fuel, keeping extra sweets and treats to a minimum, you won't be playing catch-up with exercise just to burn off what you've eaten. In other words, when you're eating well, you won't feel as if you have to exercise to purge that 550-calorie milk shake you had after school (the equivalent, by the way, of running six miles or mowing the lawn for two and a half hours). When we keep our eating habits under control, fitness becomes something we can do for fun instead of a "have to" so we won't get fat.

As simple as it sounds, eating just the calories we need in healthy forms is revolutionary to our bodies, physically and emotionally. Trust me, I know. See, I spent a whole lot of years playing this impossible game of purging the empty calories I was eating by long runs and rigorous workouts. I felt I had to burn, calorie for calorie, everything I ate. E-V-E-R-Y-T-H-I-N-G. Technically, that's called "exercise bulimia." I call it oppressive, depressing, and needlessly painful! But once I changed my relationship with food and started eating for fuel, I started to enjoy exercise more because I didn't have to do so much of it. It was no longer a punishment for what I ate but rather a fun way to make my body strong. Once my eating was in a healthy place, I started to recognize and appreciate all the best benefits of exercise.

The Benefits of Exercise

God made our bodies to move. If He wanted us to sit in one place all day like a bump on a log, He would have *made* us a bump on a log. He can do that sort of thing: He's God. Our Creator could have made us any way He wanted to, which means He designed our bodies with natural mobility on purpose. He wanted us to be able to bend, lift, run, swing, walk, hop, slide, jump, push, crouch, dance, jog, stretch, climb, swim, pull, and play. The first benefit of exercise is simply knowing and taking advantage of what you're capable of doing!

Besides helping you look your best, there are a ton of other practical reasons to make your body move. Here are just a few:[2]

- Exercise builds endurance and muscle strength. That means you can take an impromptu hike with friends without fear of passing out. You'll also have more energy and think more clearly in class.
- It helps build and maintain bones, muscles, and joints, which in turn means you'll get injured less often and have fewer aches and pains as you age. That might not sound like a huge deal now, but just you wait, missy! Old age aches start way before you think they should (not that I know anything about that).
- Exercise enhances flexibility and promotes better posture. A girl with great posture is seen as confident and capable.

- It lowers the risk of dangerous health conditions such as heart disease, colon cancer, hypertension (high blood pressure), and type 2 diabetes. Again, those might not sound threatening to you now, but they are among the most common causes of death in the United States.
- Exercise reduces stress. It can also minimize feelings of depression and anxiety and improve self-esteem and feelings of well-being. There's nothing like a good run to release all sorts of endorphins, which are better—and healthier—than any other coping substance.
- In a nutshell, regular exercise helps you live a longer, healthier, happier life!

Any of these benefits is reason enough to get moving, but there's one more really cool benefit of exercise I think you'll appreciate. I stumbled upon it while a friend of mine, Holly, and I were enjoying one of our favorite summer pastimes. Holly was part of the band that was leading worship at the summer camp where we both worked. It was a stressful job—having to look cute, sound perfect, and avoid all the boys who were dying to ask her out—so I'd steal her away to relax every so often. That particular day, we had taken our canoe out on the lake. After rowing out a ways, we took a break to just float along and enjoy the sunshine.

It was quiet for a minute or two, and then she said, "Jessie, I can already tell a difference."

"Hmmm?" I tried to wake up from my half-comatose state. "In what?"

She replied in a cheery voice, "I just started exercising again this week, and I can already tell that my legs are in better shape."

I looked over at the thigh she was admiring, and it looked the *exact same* to me! It was beautiful before, and it looked beautiful now. But she was convinced that it was different. To her, it *felt* different, and it felt good.

Holly had stumbled upon one of the great phenomena of physical activity: Even if no one else on God's green earth can tell a difference, you will. From the first time you walk or run or bike or play soccer, you will begin to feel better about yourself and your body. Long before your pants feel loose, you will be walking taller. Even before others admire your progress, you will sense a change. When we take care of our bodies, we gain confidence we wouldn't have otherwise. This might just be the biggest benefit of exercise as it relates to feeling beautiful, because . . . well, exercising *makes you feel beautiful*!

Battling the Excuses

So, given all these amazing benefits to staying physically fit, what keeps you from getting out and taking advantage of this marvelously mobile body God has given you?

If you're like me, there's a good chance that "lack of time" is at least part of your answer. It's sadly true: Most of us keep so busy that carving out even twenty minutes a day for exercise seems next to impossible. But here's a hard truth: We make time for the things we want to do. If exercise is a high enough priority to us, we'll find the time. Take a few minutes to think about the coming week. Write down five ways you can fit exercise into your routine. They can be as simple as walking around your school campus during lunch or as committed as a five-day workout plan. Up to you. Just start somewhere!

1.

2.

3.

4.

5.

The second-most-common excuse I hear is that exercise is boring. If that's your perception, forget those images you have of mat-toting, spandex-wearing, half-comatose, elliptical-riding gym rats. Exercise can be downright fun!

Here's a list of physical activities that—at least in my opinion—sound way more fun than watching TV after school.[3] Put a star next to any that you already do. Circle any activities you'd like to try. (You can even go back and add them to your exercise list!)

Moderate Activities	Vigorous Activities
Archery	Backpacking, mountain climbing
Bicycling on level terrain	Bicycling on steep terrain
Boxing a punching bag	Brisk roller or in-line skating
Canoeing or kayaking	Cross-country skiing
Dancing:	Dancing:
Ballet	Aerobic
Ballroom	Ballroom, professional
Folk	Tap
Line	Hip-hop
Contemporary	Jazz
Square	Downhill skiing
Fencing	Horseback riding, competitive
Gardening	Ice-skating, speed skating
Leisurely roller-skating or in-line skating	Jumping jacks
Hiking	Jumping rope
Horseback riding, general	Martial arts:
Juggling	Karate
Jumping on a trampoline	Judo
Leisurely ice skating	Tae kwon do
Light downhill skiing	Jujitsu
Moderate housework	Pilates
Playing with children	Playing:
	Basketball

Moderate Activities	Vigorous Activities
Playing:	Playing:
Badminton	Football
Doubles tennis	Handball
Drums or guitar in a rock band	Hockey
In a marching band	Lacrosse
Table tennis	Polo
Volleyball	Soccer
Putting away groceries	Tennis
Skateboarding	Water polo
Snorkeling	Rappelling
Snowmobiling	Rock climbing
Surfing, board or body	Running or jogging
Throwing a Frisbee	Scuba diving
Waterskiing	Swimming

Who would have thought that exercise could be so fun? Can you think of any other physical activities you might enjoy doing on a regular basis?

You might be asking, *Just how often do I have to jump rope or unpack groceries to get and stay in shape?* Expert opinions vary on how often and for how long teens should exercise. It seems the general consensus, though, is to engage in vigorous physical activity (the right-hand list) for at least thirty minutes a day, three or more times a week. Jessie's opinion? If you focus on eating right in combination with exercise, just have fun with it. Don't stress over how many minutes or how vigorously you're working out. Life's too short, and there are so many bigger problems in the world to worry about. Enjoy whatever exercise you like best as often as you can while keeping a balance with all the other stuff you have going on in your life.

Running for the Gold

To help you find your own personal balance between focusing too much on exercise and not enough, chew on this verse:

> Physical training is good, but training for godliness
> is much better, promising benefits in this life and in
> the life to come.
>
> 1 TIMOTHY 4:8

If we combine all the verses we've looked at so far, an important truth comes into focus: God cares about how we take care of our bodies, and He is even more passionate that we take care of our souls. Scripture doesn't give us one without the other, but if the physical and spiritual sides of beauty were side by side on one of those old-fashioned balance scales, the spiritual side would definitely win out. God knows that our earthly bodies, along with their beauty, last about as long as spring flowers in a hot desert (see Isaiah 40:6-8). That's why He gently reminds us that the eternal state of our souls is more important than having killer abs. First Corinthians 9:24-27 says,

You've all been to the stadium and seen the athletes race. Everyone runs; one wins. Run to win. All good athletes train hard. They do it for a gold medal that tarnishes and fades. You're after one that's gold eternally.

I don't know about you, but I'm running hard for the finish line. I'm giving it everything I've got. No sloppy living for me! I'm staying alert and in top condition. I'm not going to get caught napping, telling everyone else all about it and then missing out myself. (MSG)

Paul encourages us to live the Christian life as if we're trying to win the gold medal in the final heat at the Olympics. In order to compete at the Olympic level, you have to be in great physical condition. And in order to be in tip-top spiritual condition, you're going to have to train hard in God's gym. As we exercise our spiritual muscles, eternal rewards await.

So get that body moving. Take advantage of all those benefits of physical exercise we talked about. Your body will thank you! And while you're spending time getting those arms and quads strong, work on your spiritual physique too, because you can take that with you into eternity.

God, thank You for creating my body with the ability to move and play. I want to take care of this body You've given me. I want to experience the best this life has to offer, including good health. Jesus, You are the author of my faith.

Give me the strength to run this spiritual race well as I keep my eyes fixed on You. Amen.

Discussion Questions

1. Why do you think some girls take such an extreme stance on exercise, either for or against? Do you think it might have something to do with misconceptions about fitness?

2. Do you struggle with either of the two extremes I described: making fitness an idol or ignoring it altogether? Explain.

3. Do you tend to exercise out of guilt over your food choices?

4. How do you think your view of exercise might change as you put into practice the things you learned about healthy eating in Step #7?

5. *Write about a time when you were physically active and felt better about yourself and your body even before there were any physical changes.*

6. *What lifestyle changes do you need to make in order to stick to a healthy exercise routine? (For example, you might decide to limit your TV viewing to a half hour a day or commit to finding a friend who will exercise with you.)*

7. *In what ways can a Christian girl train so she'll be in even better shape spiritually than she is physically? Which of those ways do you need to work on in your life?*

Treat Your Scale like a Magic Mirror

DIRECTIONS: If you want to feel terrible about your weight, buy a scale and put it in a place where you'll remember to weigh yourself often. Get on that puppy morning and night and ask whether you're "the lightest of them all." Make sure to obsess over any changes you see on the display, regardless of water weight, growth, or PMS.

I wasn't a huge fan of Disney's *Snow White* as a kid. (Sorry, Snow, but *Sleeping Beauty* was my absolute favorite.) Even though I didn't like the movie all that much, I have to say there were parts of it that were way memorable. Anyone who has ever watched *Snow White* will remember the little dwarfs singing "Heigh-Ho" and the creepy old lady with the poison apple. Those scenes stick in our brains like gum to a locker. And among the most impossible to forget is the Magic Mirror scene. Can you picture it? Inside the castle, the tall, hooded queen walks slowly up the steps to her mirror and recites a chant to summon the Slave in the Magic Mirror from the farthest space, through wind and darkness, yada yada. After some lightning, fire, and creepy music, that freaky hollow face appears. (And I'm suddenly reminded why I didn't like this movie. Can you say *nightmares?*) The face asks her what she would like to know, and the queen answers with perhaps the most famous words of the entire movie: "Magic Mirror on the wall, who is the fairest one of all?" And we all know the rest of the story.

This scene reveals a lot about the movie's antagonist. Not only is the queen intimidating, evil, and a bit tweeze happy on those needle-thin eyebrows, she also has some serious insecurity issues. I mean, who bases their entire happiness on the report of a mirror? Most people would be happy enough to have "famed beauty" and get to run the entire kingdom, but not this queen. She won't be satisfied unless she hears what she wants to hear from that mirror. Now, that just sounds petty, doesn't it? But before we're too hard on the queen, let's ask ourselves a hard question:

Are we any different?

So many of us begin each day climbing on our real-life version of that Magic Mirror, practically begging it to tell us what we want to hear. "Scale, scale, on my floor, tell me I'm lighter than the day before. Pretty *pleeeease?*" And just like the queen with the insecurity issues, we have our own little fit when we don't like the number we see. *What?! Two pounds heavier? Ugh!!!* Some of us let that news ruin the rest of our day, or we punish ourselves by restricting food or talking down to ourselves with just-plain-mean words.

I call it the Magic Mirror syndrome (or MMS for short).

MMS really is completely illogical when you think about

it. Why should we base our entire day's happiness on a square-foot box of metal and plastic doohickeys? A scale can't weigh a person's talents, dreams, personality, relationships, or intelligence. A scale can't weigh beauty, and it certainly can't put a number on worth, but do you pretend that it can?

Do you base your happiness, worth, or beauty on a number? If you're not sure, this little quiz might help you find out:

"MAGIC MIRROR SYNDROME" QUIZ

1. *How often do you weigh yourself?*
   A. Every day
   B. Once a week
   C. Only at the doctor's office
   D. More than once a day

2. *If you got on the scale today and the number was five pounds higher than the last time you got on the scale, you would*
   A. Shed a tear (possibly many)
   B. Go for a long run
   C. Shrug it off
   D. Punish yourself in some way (not eating, cutting, etc.)

3. *When you have to tell others what you weigh (such as for a sports roster or a driver's license), you*
   A. Lie, point-blank
   B. Tell the truth but wonder what others will think
   C. Tell the truth and don't sweat it
   D. Get serious anxiety and then lie

4. *The thought of not weighing yourself for one month sounds*

   A. Kind of hard

   B. Freeing

   C. Like not a big deal

   D. Impossible

Again, no scoring necessary. I have a feeling that as you answered the questions, you already got a sense of whether you're living in freedom or enslaved to your weight.

I think it's time for us smart girls to start acting smart and really think through why we place so much importance on those numbers on the scale. As someone who was chained to the report I'd get from my bathroom scale (aka, my own personal Magic Mirror) for a very long time, I'm happy to share that there's a better way.

Christ Came for Freedom

Do you know why Jesus came to earth? Why would a being who is everything, has everything, and created everything become a roughly eight-pound mass of human cells and DNA, tied down by space and time, and subject to sickness, sin, and sand in His sandals? It's kind of crazy to think about, isn't it? Something was so important to Jesus that He laid His God-ness aside and became human (see Philippians 2:6-8).

So what was it?

First Timothy 1:15 gives us the "Sunday school" answer:

"Christ Jesus came into the world to save sinners." But if you dig a little deeper and wider through the New Testament, you start to see an even bigger picture unfold. As we read about Jesus' reasons for dying, we often see a word I really love: freedom.

Yes, Jesus died to save us from the penalty of going to hell because of our sin (see Romans 3:24), but He also set us free from the *power* of sin (see Romans 6:7), the *ownership* of sin (see Romans 6:18, 20), and the *prison* of sin (see Galatians 3:22). The reason Jesus left heaven and spent thirty-three years on this wacky planet was to offer us freedom. And if that's true, we'd be crazy not to take advantage of it! That's why Paul said,

> Christ has truly set us free. Now *make sure that you stay free*, and don't get tied up again in slavery. . . . For *you have been called to live in freedom*, my brothers and sisters.
> GALATIANS 5:1, 13, EMPHASIS ADDED

Newsflash: Christ busted the door clean off our jail cell when He beat death. Freedom is ours for the taking! But Jesus doesn't force us to live in freedom; we have to make that choice. We can either live like the free girls we are or hang out in our dungeons of self-hate and idol worship. I don't know about you, but standing on my scale each morning did *not* help me live in freedom. (Big surprise, right?) Instead, it imprisoned me. More specifically, it took my focus off God and serving others and made me completely preoccupied with how many ounces I had gained or lost that day. I was chained to my scale. I was bowing down to a different god than the One who came for my freedom.

If we're going to understand and appreciate our true beauty, we have to stop spending so much energy and emotion on those blasted scales. We have to get to a place where we want freedom from every hindrance, including weight obsession, so badly that we'll do whatever it takes to live like the free girls we are.

A Story of Freedom

A friend of mine, Mandy Ballard, got to that place. I have nothing but admiration for this beautiful chick because of the brave step she took to "stay free"! Here's Mandy's story in her own words:

> *I eat really well at home, but if I'm at a party or a dinner out with my husband, my rule is to eat and enjoy. And I do! So back in early August, we had all kinds of parties and things to go to. After a few parties and events—ahem—I had gained a couple of pounds. I expected it. But you know what? Every morning I weighed myself, and it made me upset.*
>
> *Really, though, who cares about two or three pounds? I did.*
>
> *And I let it get to me.*
>
> *My morning weight often affected my emotions for the rest of the day. But one morning was different.*

I stepped on the scale as usual and scoffed at the number that wouldn't budge no matter what I did. As I was getting ready for the day, God whispered this to me:

> *Cast down your idol. Throw away your scale.*
> *A number on a plastic box doesn't deserve your emotions, your attention, your heart.*

It hit me like a ton of bricks.

In the name of self-discipline, I've spent years trapped by a number on a plastic box. I have spent years bowing down to my scale with my emotions. I let a number that tells me the effect gravitational force has on my body affect my soul.

Does that sound ridiculous to you, too?

My heart started beating like crazy as I imagined a world free of even knowing what I weighed. Before I could shove the idea away, the Spirit helped me embrace it.

I got rid of my scale.

For the first time in years, I don't know what I weigh.

My scale was only one little idol, but it had a big part of my life. I know that Satan had a stronghold in my life because of it. I sometimes still want to go buy a new one and forget I ever took it out! That's how ingrained weighing myself was in my life. But God was gracious to me and let me see what it was doing to me. I was making it a god.

The truth is, I can be healthy—while losing or gaining weight—and I don't need a number to tell me that's happening.

Getting rid of my scale was really hard for me. It would have been impossible two years ago. But God is so good that He made it easy. I wanted to do it, because where the Spirit of the Lord is, there is freedom. The chains of sin are broken! And I want to live in freedom.[1]

The Scale-less Experiment

I love Mandy's story because it represents yet another girl's journey toward ever-increasing freedom. I hope that's a journey you're on too: stopping every so often to figure out what's holding you back from complete freedom and chucking those things to the curb. It's a process, isn't it? We think we're good, we're holy, we're doing our thing, and then God taps us on the shoulder and points to the giant sin hitching a ride on our hearts and—sometimes gently, sometimes by handing us a hacksaw—pushes us to cut it off so we can run our "race" well (see Hebrews 12:1-2). He wants us to live the beautiful, free lives He died to give us.

Sometimes the sin in our lives is obvious, and sometimes we don't see it even when it's right under our noses. When it comes to our scales, I think the latter is usually true. Most of us don't realize how devoted we are to the scale idol until we give it up, so I'm going to ask you to do something—something brave, something courageous, something that might make your friends and family think you're loony.

Give up your scale—wait for it—for *one whole year*.

If that sounds impossible, let me assure you that you will not die. You won't blow up like a balloon, and you certainly won't quit functioning throughout the day. In fact, you just might find that without your scale, you can function a whole lot better! So take your scale off its shrine and chuck it, smash it, or pack it in a box in the attic for three hundred sixty-five days. I don't care what you do with it as long as you don't stand on it.

Your assignment, should you choose to accept it, is to record your scale-less adventure in your journal. Explain why you're doing it and what you hope to accomplish. Write about how you feel that first day . . . the forty-seventh . . . the three-hundredth. Celebrate every little victory of freedom. And how much more fun would this be with a friend? I highly encourage you to recruit a partner (or a team) to accompany you on this mission! (You'll find shareable images at www.LifeLoveandGod.com/backwards-beauty.)

Participating in this little scale-less experiment isn't going to earn you bonus "God points" or make you a super-Christian. However, you just might experience that freedom we talked about earlier—the freedom Mandy and I have found, the freedom Christ died to give you.

It's funny—do you know I used to weigh myself every

day? I would hold my breath while waiting for the numbers to calculate and light up the digital display. Now though? Since I stopped consulting my Magic Mirror every single day, I hardly think about my weight (or, consequently, my size). I honestly can't remember the last time I stepped on my scale! That overrated weighing machine now collects dust in my bathroom closet, just like those once-familiar insecurities collecting dust in a forgotten corner of my heart.

Insecurities melt in the warmth of freedom.

Maybe someone should explain that to the queen.

Father, You are the only God—not my size, not my weight, not my scale—who deserves my devotion. You are it! Forgive me for giving so much of my energy and emotions to that stuff. I want to live in the freedom You died to give me—not just the freedom to be more than a number but the freedom to be more than I am now as You change and grow me. Give me strength to move past my idols. Amen.

Discussion Questions

1. What is the Magic Mirror syndrome?

2. *Why is it silly to base our happiness, worth, or beauty on a number? Why do you think we're tempted to do it anyway?*

3. *Name five things a scale can't measure:*
   a.
   b.
   c.
   d.
   e.

4. *According to Galatians 5:1, 13, who set you free? Who is responsible for you to stay free?*

5. *Are you going to take the one-year scale-less challenge? Why or why not?*

Idolize Beauty

DIRECTIONS: Make physical beauty the end-all, highest goal of your life. Everyone says that if you're gorgeous, you'll be happier and more successful and get the man of your dreams, so forget about the beauty that comes from your heart and especially the beauty that comes from Christ *in* you. Serving God and His Kingdom can wait until you've reached mirror perfection.

Say *what?!* My jaw almost hit the floor. When you read this headline, it just might grab your attention too:

**Italian Woman, 85, Ends Her Life Because
She Was Upset about Losing Her Looks**

Seriously? Yeah, seriously. Apparently Oriella Cazzanello couldn't handle wrinkles taking over her once youthful, beautiful face. The article included a picture. No, Oriella might not have been twenty anymore, but she was actually a very lovely Italian grandmother. The kind of soft, wrinkly lovely that makes you want to nuzzle in for a big hug and a kiss on both slightly sagging cheeks. She didn't see herself as lovely though. She had a picture of "beautiful" in her mind, and because she didn't match it, depression set in.

Eventually—without even telling her family—she traveled to a clinic in Basel, Switzerland, where she spent 10,000 euros to end her life—over her looks.[1] True story.

There's a reason that headline made news: It's nuts! And I'm thankful that most of the world's population still thinks so. It's not as though people are lining up to die because they aren't pretty enough. But even though Oriella's story sounds extreme, the beauty-obsessed road we're traveling on might take us dangerously close to that cliff if we're not careful.

When I read Oriella's story, I found myself wondering, *How does someone get to the place where they'd choose death rather than "suffer through" wrinkles, flab, and varicose veins?* If we live long enough, *all* of us are going to "lose our looks," at least by the media's definition. Beauty (as the world understands it) lasts about as long as a snowflake on your tongue (see Proverbs 31:30), and if we place our hope and happiness in it, we're going to be sorely disappointed in the end! I think that's what happened to poor Oriella. She had spent her life clinging to her beauty, and when that beauty faded, she had nothing left to live for.

Those of us in generations X, Y, and Z might not be ready to die over our looks just yet, but we're on our way there, sadly. Obsession leads to depression, and as Oriella found, depression leads to desperation. And the journey to that cliff starts by making beauty into an idol.

The Making of an Idol

Just so we're on the same page, let's talk a minute about what makes an idol an idol. Here's my one-sentence summary of Isaiah 44: An idol is anything (1) made that (2) takes God's rightful place as the number one priority in our lives.

By that definition, aren't we guilty of letting all sorts of idols take over our hearts? Everything (guys, music, social media, clothes, sports) can take on idol status if we're not careful. God knows how quickly we replace Him with just about anything and everything. That's why He dedicated not just one but two of the Ten Commandments to warning us against idolatry:

> You must not have any other god but me.
>   You must not make for yourself an idol of any
> kind or an image of anything in the heavens or on
> the earth or in the sea. You must not bow down
> to them or worship them, for I, the LORD your
> God, am a jealous God who will not tolerate your
> affection for any other gods.
>
> EXODUS 20:3-5

An idol is anything in our lives that takes God's rightful place as numero uno—anything that we bow down to in our hearts. If we put our hope in our looks, spend too much time on our looks, or let our happiness rise and fall over our looks, then we've made beauty an idol.

You know, God hasn't given us a single rule just for the

heck of it. He knows our hearts better than anyone else, and He knows how easily we chase after all sorts of things that would end up hurting us. He gives us commands that are only for our good (and His glory). The command to have no other gods besides Him is a perfect example. He knows that if we chase them, idols will destroy us. Psalm 16:4 says, "Troubles multiply for those who chase after other gods."

When we make beauty a god, boy do our troubles multiply! Bowing to the beauty idol makes us live like prisoners. I'm guessing you know what I'm talking about here. It's exhausting to make sure our hair has enough bounce, our tummy has enough "packs," and our skin is just the right shade of bronze. We wear ourselves out worrying about how many pounds we weigh, whether our chest is big enough, and how our thighs look in our leggings—not to mention the shackles of comparison, jealousy, and pride.

Yep—when beauty is our idol, we serve a cruel master.

God doesn't want His daughters to live in chains! Jesus died for our freedom, remember? We talked about that freedom in the previous chapter. Christ has busted the doors off of our jail cells, but we have the responsibility to stay free.

I know it's not easy. Man, do I know! For all the reasons we've talked about in this book—the media, the temptation to compare, our pride, and our desire to be desired—getting free of our beauty prison ain't easy! But it is doable. We can do all things, even casting down our beauty idol, through Jesus who gives us the strength to do God's will (see Philippians 4:13).

Melting the Mirrors . . . Literally

There were some girls a long, long time ago who decided to break free from the beauty idol. To hear the story, we're going to take a little field trip to the Pentateuch (the first five books of the Bible).

The Israelites had spent a whole lot of years in Egypt (four hundred, give or take) when God sent Moses to free them from slavery. Pharaoh had a wicked stubborn streak; God had to send plague after plague to convince him to let His people go. When God sent the final plague on Egypt—the night Pharaoh lost his son and finally told them to get out of Dodge NOW!—the Israelite women didn't have much time to pack. God had told them to have their walking shoes by the door and be ready to go at a moment's notice. So everyone packed the essentials: a bit of food, some gifts from Egyptian neighbors—oh, and a mirror. Of course. What self-respecting girl *wouldn't* pack a mirror for a perilous night-time escape into the wilderness? (Just goes to show you that girls were pretty much the same 3,500 years ago as we are today.) By golly, those heavy bronze mirrors traveled across the Red Sea, through the wilderness, all the way to the foot of Mount Sinai.

Now, no one would go through that much trouble to make sure she had a mirror in the desert unless she *really* liked her mirror. And I think it's safe to say that anyone *that* into her mirror probably cared a lot about her looks.

Can you relate? Personally, I really can't blame them for

taking their mirrors on a trans-desert journey. Example #1: I'm a total makeup camper. No shower? No big deal. But don't think for a moment I won't pack my mascara! Example #2: I have a mirror in just about every room in my house. The thought of going who knows how long without looking into one is a wee bit frightening. What if my hair looked frizzy? How would I tweeze my eyebrows or apply my treasured mascara? For heaven's sake, how would I pick at my pimples?! I can't imagine a world without at least one mirror in it, though I really wish that weren't true. Sadly, I don't think I'm alone.

That's what makes the next part of the story so inspiring.

There at the base of Mount Sinai, Moses explained that God wanted them to build a tent of meeting (or tabernacle) for God to live in. The Tabernacle would be portable so they could take it with them through the wilderness. That way, God would always be close to them, even while they took the forty-year "scenic route" to the Promised Land.

To create the Tabernacle, they were going to need a lot of supplies: gold, silver, fabric, wood, thread, leather, oil, and spices. The Israelites rummaged through the bounty they had brought from Egypt and gave generously to get that tent built. But there's one particular gift worth noting. Remember those bronze mirrors? We find them here in Exodus 38:8:

> Bezalel made the bronze washbasin and its bronze
> stand from bronze mirrors donated by the women
> who served at the entrance of the Tabernacle.

In an act of complete selflessness, some of the Israelite women gave up their mirrors for God. Not all, but some. Did you notice which ones? The women who chose to give up their mirrors were those who served God at the entrance to the Tabernacle. Reading between the lines, I'm guessing that as those women served God day after day, their hearts were changed. The mirrors that seemed all-important back in Egypt weren't so necessary anymore. As they spent time in God's presence, they slowly began to see themselves through His eyes. They didn't need a mirror to judge their beauty because they had purpose and joy and freedom in serving Him!

I see you sweating. Don't worry, I'm not going to ask you to give up your mirror for a year too. (But by all means, listen to the Holy Spirit if He does ask!)

I share this story because that tiny passage, tucked in between pages of rules and regulations, gives me such hope as a girl! If they were able to break free from the beauty idol, so can we. And the best part is that now, because of the new covenant through Jesus, we don't need a tabernacle to be close to God. We *are* the temple, remember? God's Spirit lives in us, and because He does, we can be changed into God's image a little more each day.

The Most Beautiful Thing about You

From the very start, I've wanted this book to be honest. I'm not a fan of pat answers that don't allow room for real-life struggles.

So in the nature of honesty, I'm going to say something that might sound as though it contradicts everything I've written so far:

You'll probably always care about how you look.

I wish it weren't so, but that's just how it is. The combination of our God-given humanness and sin (which isn't going anywhere anytime soon) pretty much ensures that we're not going to *completely* erase our desire to like what we see when we look in a mirror. Here's the cool part, though, and why I'm okay living with that tension: The longer we die to sin and live in Jesus' light, the *less* we'll care about our looks and the *more* we'll care about Him and His Kingdom. The longer we follow Jesus, learn from Him, and become like Him, the more we live out this truth:

God > My Beauty

When we run hard after God, He shows us how to both desire beauty and let it go—*at the same time.*

The closer we get to Jesus, the more we'll understand that God will always be greater than our physical beauty. And the closer we get to Jesus, the more we discover that the most beautiful parts of us aren't on the outside at all. If we're serving the true God, we'll only get more beautiful with time. Girl, by the time we're eighty-five, we're going to be the most truly beautiful of our lives! We'll be looking forward to death, not so we can ditch our wrinkly, sagging booties like the Italian granny but so we can stare into the eyes of our Savior—the One who gave us a beauty that doesn't age or fade. And then, at the resurrection, we're going to have brand-new, A-M-A-Z-I-N-G bodies that will leave these sacks of bones in the dust. Can someone give me an amen?! Someday you will have the best body ever! How 'bout that for something to look forward to?

In the chapter about the danger of comparing ourselves to others, I had you step out of your comfort zone (and bust out your artistic skills) to draw and label five things about your body that are uniquely beautiful. Now I want you to dig even deeper and think about those beautiful things about you that no one can see with their eyes. What are five—no make

that *ten*—of the most beautiful things about you? Don't worry, I'll go first. (This doesn't classify as boasting because anything good in our hearts is 100 percent God's doing!)

Despite my best efforts at helping you feel ugly, I'm afraid my ten steps may have backfired. I tried to help you feel miserable about yourself. Really, I did. But at the end of the day, there's just no denying the truth:

You. Are. Beautiful.

Inside and out.

Embrace that beauty, find joy in that beauty, stand tall in that beauty. Just don't *idolize* your beauty. Live in the freedom Jesus died to give you! Because of Him, you're . . .

Free to be you—*imperfect* you.

Free to enjoy your beauty and the beauty around you.

Free to love God with everything you are.

God, forgive me for serving beauty like an idol. You're the only One who deserves to sit on the throne in my heart. I want to live the free life Jesus died to give me. So as I serve You with my life, God, would You open my eyes to see just how beautiful I am, inside and out? I want to be a reflection of Your indescribable beauty! I love You. Amen.

Discussion Questions

1. *What is an idol?*

2. *How can the quest for physical beauty become an idol in our hearts?*

3. *Has it become one in yours? How can you tell?*

4. *Why is it actually in our best interest to get rid of our idols?*

5. *Do you think you'll always care about how you look to some degree? Explain.*

6. *Pull out your journal one more time. Take a few minutes to write your own prayer to God, thanking Him for the beautiful way He made you, and asking Him to help your heart become more and more beautiful with time.*

Notes

START HERE: KALE, KATE, AND THE GREAT LONGING

1. The facts presented in this chart are a mixture of personal observation and multiple sources, including Dr. James Dobson's Family Talk, "Physical Differences between Men and Women," http://drjames dobson.org/Solid-Answers/Answers?a=ff773023-2693-410d-b9e1 -662f6985be4e; Nastasia Peters, "The Differences between Male and Female Portraits," http://design.tutsplus.com/articles/the-differences -between-male-and-female-portraits--vector-14954; University of New South Wales, "Why Do Women Store Fat Differently from Men?" *ScienceDaily*, www.sciencedaily.com/releases/2009/03/090302115755 .htm; Andrea Cespedes, "Amount of Muscle Mass in Men Versus Women," last updated May 5, 2015, *Livestrong*, http://www.livestrong .com/article/246036-how-much-more-muscle-mass-does-a-male-have -than-a-female/; and Gettysburg College, "Why Cosmetics Work: More Depth to Facial Differences between Men and Women than Presumed," *ScienceDaily*, www.sciencedaily.com/releases/2009/10 /091020153100.htm.

2. Eve wasn't created only for Adam's pleasure; she was created to glorify God and enjoy Him forever, just as Adam was. But for the purposes of this book, I've intentionally focused on the unique nature of her physical and emotional beauty.

3. Name has been changed. Story used with permission.

4. Focus on the Family, *Created Beautiful* (Ventura, CA: Gospel Light, 2005).

STEP #1: BELIEVE WHAT YOU SEE ON SCREEN

1. *Seventeen*, March 2014 issue.

2. Louise Story, "Anywhere the Eye Can See, It's Likely to See an Ad," *New York Times*, January 15, 2007, http://www.nytimes.com/2007 /01/15/business/media/15everywhere.html?pagewanted=all&_r=0.

3. Ibid.
4. Eric Pfanner, "A Move to Curb Digitally Altered Photos in Ads," *New York Times*, September 27, 2009, http://www.nytimes.com /2009/09/28/business/media/28brush.html.
5. Dove Films, "Evolution," 2006.
6. Alanna Vagianos, "Survey Proves We Still Really Need to Talk about Photoshop," *Huffington Post*, November 27, 2013.
7. Ibid.
8. *Merriam-Webster's Collegiate Dictionary*, 11th ed., s.v. "model."
9. If you're not familiar with the way God created Eve out of one of Adam's ribs, see Genesis 2:21-22.

STEP #2: GET "THE LOOK" AT ALL COSTS

1. "Jessica Simpson's The Price of Beauty," VH1, episode 101, first aired March 12, 2010.
2. "Pots of Promise: An Industry Driven by Sexual Instinct Will Always Thrive," *Economist*, May 22, 2003, http://www.economist.com/node /1795852.
3. *Wikipedia*, "Wasp Waist," accessed February 27, 2014, http://en .wikipedia.org/wiki/Wasp_waist.
4. "Chinese Foot Binding," *BBC*, accessed March 2, 2014, http://www .bbc.co.uk/dna/ptop/alabaster/A1155872.
5. "Jessica Simpson's The Price of Beauty," VH1, episode 106, first aired April 20, 2010.
6. "Jessica Simpson's The Price of Beauty," VH1, episode 104, first aired April 6, 2010.
7. "Jessica Simpson's The Price of Beauty," VH1, episode 101, first aired March 12, 2010; and "The Karen People," The Peoples of the World Foundation (2002), retrieved March 2, 2014, http://www .peoplesoftheworld.org/text?people=Karen.
8. "South Korean Girls' Obsession with Double Eyelid Surgery as They Strive to Look like 'Pretty Western Celebrities,'" *Daily Mail*, accessed March 2, 2014, http://www.dailymail.co.uk/femail/article-2222481 /South-Korean-girls-obsession-double-eyelid-surgery-strive-look-like -pretty-western-celebrities.html.
9. AnnaMaria Andriotis, "10 Things the Beauty Industry Won't Tell You," *Market Watch*, April 20, 2011, http://www.marketwatch.com /story/10-things-the-beauty-industry-wont-tell-you-1303249279432.
10. "Jessica Simpson's The Price of Beauty," VH1, episode 107, first aired April 27, 2010.

11. Megan Segura, "How Much Time We Really Spend on Beauty," *Daily Makeover*, accessed March 2, 2014, http://www.dailymakeover.com /trends/makeup/time-spent-on-beauty/.
12. Ian O'Neill, "How Long Does It Take to Get to the Moon?" *Universe Today*, November 7, 2013, http://www.universetoday.com/13562 /how-long-does-it-take-to-get-to-the-moon/.
13. David Jeannot, "Women Spend $125,000 on Clothes over Lifetime: Study," *NBC 6 South Florida*, July 5, 2012, http://www.nbcmiami.com /news/local/Women-Spend-125000-on-Clothes-Over-Lifetime-Study -161496035.html.
14. Ross Crooks, "Splurge vs. Save: Which Beauty Products Are Worth the Extra Cost?" *MintLife*, April 11, 2013, https://www.mint.com/blog /consumer-iq/splurge-vs-save-which-beauty-products-are-worth-the -extra-cost-0413/?display=wide.
15. Lolita A. Alford, "The World Spends Billions to Look Beautiful," *FashInvest*, April 19, 2013, http://www.fashinvest.com/world-spends -billions-beautiful-big-beauty-industry/.

STEP #4: BELIEVE NASTY WORDS (YOURS AND OTHERS')

1. All verses in this section are paraphrased from the New Living Translation.
2. James Strong, *The New Strong's Exhaustive Concordance of the Bible* (Nashville: Thomas Nelson, 2001), Hebrew word #2580.

STEP #5: REFUSE TO TAKE A COMPLIMENT

1. Richard Glover, "Oh, You Beautiful Blokes, if Only Anna Could See through Our Eyes," *Sydney Morning Herald*, June 22, 2002. Used with permission.
2. From e-mail interview. Used with permission.

STEP #6: VIEW YOUR BODY AS A POWER TOOL

1. *Seventeen*, March 2014 issue.

STEP #7: EAT JUNK AND DIET, DIET, DIET

1. Centers for Disease Control and Prevention, *Obesity and Overweight Statistics for 2009-10*, accessed April 16, 2014, http://www.cdc.gov /nchs/fastats/overwt.htm.
2. Cynthia L. Ogden, Margaret D. Carroll, Brian K. Kit, and Katherine M. Flegal, "Prevalence of Childhood and Adult Obesity in the United States, 2011–2012," *Journal of the American Medical Association* (2014), 311(8): 806–814.

3. World Health Organization, "Obesity and Overweight, Fact Sheet No. 311," updated March 2013, http://www.who.int/mediacentre/factsheets/fs311/en/.

4. Lysa TerKeurst and Shaunti Feldhahn, *Made to Crave for Young Women: Satisfying Your Deepest Desires with* God (Grand Rapids, MI: Zonderkidz, 2012).

STEP #8: ADORE OR IGNORE EXERCISE

1. Our body's energy system is more complex than calories in, calories out. For example, our bodies digest and metabolize types of food differently. A body treats 120 calories of apple differently than 120 calories of Skittles, so viewing our bodies like calorie calculators isn't exactly accurate. But generally, we can expect that if we consistently eat more calories than our bodies use, we will pack on extra weight.

2. Adapted from United States Department of Agriculture, "Why Is Physical Activity Important?" accessed July 18, 2006, http://choose myplate.gov/physical-activity-why.

3. Adapted from B. E. Ainsworth, W. L. Haskell, and A. S. Leon, "Compendium of Physical Activities: Classification of Energy Costs of Human Physical Activities," *Medicine and Science in Sports and Exercise* (1993) 25(1): 71–80, http://www.cdc.gov/nccdphp/dnpa/physical/pdf/PA_Intensity_table_2_1.pdf.

STEP #9: TREAT YOUR SCALE LIKE A MAGIC MIRROR

1. Adapted from Mandy Ballard, "Smashing the Idol of the Scale," September 21, 2012, http://biblicalhomemaking.blogspot.com/2012/09/smashing-idol-of-scale.html. Used with permission. Mandy is a fitness instructor and the hostess of BiblicalHomemaking.com, where she inspires thousands of woman with godly advice, cool DIY projects, handy thrifting tips, and healthy food ideas. Pay her a visit at her website and be sure to check out her social media links!

STEP #10: IDOLIZE BEAUTY

1. Hannah Roberts, "Italian Woman, 85, Ends Her Life at Swiss Euthanasia Clinic Because She Was Upset about Losing Her Looks," *Daily Mail Online*, February 20, 2014, http://www.dailymail.co.uk/news/article-2564023/Italian-woman-85-ends-life-Swiss-Dignitas-clinic-upset-losing-looks.html?ITO=1490&ns_mchannel=rss&ns_campaign=1490.

A Note
from the Author

For ten years, I've been writing and speaking, praying with and encouraging teen girls to live in the sweet spot of God's will for their lives. I love people of both genders and all ages—and I write and speak for them too—but I have a special place in my heart for young women. It's that heartache-y passion for my little sisters that led me to launch LifeLoveandGod.com, a website where I've been answering girls' most personal questions since 2005. And it's the same passion that has led me to write, speak, and mentor teen and young women for more than ten years.

I live by the adage "My life is an open book." Sometimes that means sharing stories with an audience that should really be reserved for reality TV shows. Sometimes that means crying real tears while I type wildly at a corner table at Starbucks. God never asked me to share a shiny, cellophane-wrapped version of my life with the world, so I offer the real me with all my messy details, hoping that both my failures and triumphs will encourage you on your own faith journey.

Freedom and *grace* are two of my favorite things in life. I hope you'll find lots of both any time you pick up one of my books. Those gems also come with me when I speak (along with their awkward cousin *humor*).

I consider it the highest honor to share life with you—whether through books or on stage. If I could gather you close for a big hug, I would (and I don't even care if you're not a hugger—deal with it). I can't wait for the day we'll get to meet in person!

If you'd like to invite me to your event,
please shoot me a line at
LifeLoveandGod.com/speaking.